Also by Frances and Dorothy Wood

ANIMALS IN DANGER: THE STORY OF VANISHING AMERICAN WILDLIFE

By Frances Wood

Our National Parks Series

YELLOWSTONE, GLACIER, GRAND TETON
GRAND CANYON, ZION, BRYCE CANYON
YOSEMITE, SEQUOIA AND KINGS CANYON, HAWAII
ROCKY MOUNTAIN, MESA VERDE, CARLSBAD CAVERNS
GREAT SMOKY MOUNTAINS, EVERGLADES, MAMMOTH CAVE
MOUNT RAINIER, MOUNT MC KINLEY, OLYMPIC

Enchantment of America Series

PANORAMIC PLAINS
GULF LANDS AND CENTRAL SOUTH
LAKES, HILLS AND PRAIRIES
MEXICO

By Dorothy Wood

BEAVERS
PLANTS WITH SEEDS
LONG EYE AND THE IRON HORSE

Enchantment of America Series

SEA AND SUNSHINE
HILLS AND HARBORS
NEW ENGLAND COUNTRY
CANADA

Science Parade Series

THE BEAR FAMILY
THE CAT FAMILY

FORESTS ARE FOR PEOPLE

PEOPLE

The Heritage of Our National Forests

FRANCES and DOROTHY WOOD

Illustrated with Photographs

DODD, MEAD & COMPANY · NEW YORK

All the photographs that appear in this book are used by courtesy of the U.S. Forest Service except for the following: pages 16 and 198, the Union Pacific Railroad; pages 100 and 126, the Arkansas Game & Fish Commission; page 108 (left), the Department of the Interior, Grand Canyon National Park; pages 128-29, the Grand Junction, Colorado, *Daily Sentinel;* page 171, the Jackson Hole Ski Corporation.

Acknowledgments

The authors are grateful to many members of the National Forest Service who gave liberally of their time and energy to help us gather the information for this book. For guiding us on long trips through the forests, critically reading portions of the manuscript, and providing us with photographs, we are especially indebted to:

Henry W. DeBruin, Director of Information and Education, T. B. Glazebrook, Director of Watershed Management, Richard Mosher and Paul Steucke, all of Washington, D.C.; W. W. Huber, Southern Region; Robert A. Entzminger and Eldon G. Lucas, Tallahassee; Maxwell Wallace and Dick Pike, Ocala National Forest, Florida; Alvin McDonald and Tom O'Connor, Apalachicola National Forest, Florida; C. E. Hensen, Daniel Boone National Forest, Kentucky; Sam King, Nantahala National Forest, North Carolina; Johnsey King, Manager of the W. W. Ashe Nursery, and W. E. Showalter, DeSoto National Forest, Mississippi; Frank Finison, Forrest Carpenter, Robert M. Laval, Tom Hawks, and June O. Terry, Kisatchie National Forest, Louisiana; Eva V. Evans, Edward F. Adams, Warren O. Hilgemann, and Leonce A. Cambre, Ouachita National Forest, Arkansas and Oklahoma; J. Arthur Martin and Chuck McConnell, Grand Mesa National Forest and Uncompahgre National Forest, Colorado; Scott Phillips, Teton National Forest, Wyoming; Richard O. Benjamin and Phil Johnson, Ashley National Forest, Utah; K. A. Keeney, E. Arnold Hanson, Jud Moore, E. Del-Mar Jaquish, Northern Region, A. P. Brackebusch, Northern Forest Fire Laboratory; Paul A. Hoskins, Galatin National Forest, Montana; J. H. Wood, Merle F. Pugh, and Vic Kreimeyer, Pacific Northwest Region; Fred Heisler, Mount Hood National Forest, Oregon; W. Jane Westenberger, California Region; Jack C. Culbreath, Alaska Region; Nelson T. Bernard, Jr., Southwestern Region; Mark J. Boesch, Eastern Region; Lester T. Magnus, Superior National Forest, Minnesota; A. J. Quinkert, Nicolet National Forest, Wisconsin; and Richard E. Larson, Lower Michigan National Forests.

Many people outside the Forest Service gave us important information and their own time and effort to enhance our personal experience with the forests. Among these are Frank and Mary Alice Hansen of Tofte, Minnesota, who took us for an unforgettable canoe trip in the Boundary Waters Canoe Area of Superior National Forest, starting at Lake Sawbill; and our brother, David Wood, Jr., who supplied invaluable information and guided numerous personal visits to the forests of western Colorado.

"FOR THE GREATEST GOOD..."

"Are you a Forest Ranger?"

The district ranger turned at the question and saw two boys standing there, one about fourteen and the other only five or six.

"Yes, I am," he agreed amiably.

"My little brother wants to see a real, live Forest Ranger," the older boy explained earnestly. "Will you stand still and let him look at you?"

The ranger laughed and stood still while, from all angles, the small boy inspected him and his trim green National Forest Service uniform, with the Forest Service insignia on the left shoulder. Then the older boy nodded his thanks, and the two went happily on their way. The ranger laughed again and went his way, too, his amusement easing the burden of the many problems on his mind.

In the Forest Service, the term "ranger" is used only for the district ranger and his assistant ranger, if he has one. Each forest is divided into two or more districts, and the ranger is responsible for looking after everything that goes on in his district. He is a businessman as well as a woodsman. He must be able to direct his office and field staff and to spend the money wisely that is allocated to his district.

His superior is the forest supervisor, who is responsible for a whole forest or perhaps more than one forest. There are nine forest regions in the United States, with a regional forester and his staff in charge of each region.

We haven't always had national forests. Toward the end of

the last century, it seemed all the forests might be cut down and destroyed. Most of those in the East had already disappeared; the vast forests of the West might not, after all, last forever. A few wise leaders got together and persuaded Congress and the President to do something about it.

So the first "forest reserves" were set aside, and the Organic Act authorized their managed use. Now they are the "national forests," managed by the United States Forest Service in the Department of Agriculture. Gifford Pinchot, who had led the work to save the forests, was the first Chief of the Forest Service.

At first, all national forests came from public land, most of it in the West. But in 1911 the Weeks Law was passed permitting the purchase of land for national forests. Since then the federal government has purchased about twenty million acres for forests, nearly all of it in forty-eight national forests in the East.

We now have nearly 187 million acres in 154 national forests and 19 grasslands, in forty-one states and Puerto Rico. This is more than four times the total area of New England, and about six times the area of New York, or Pennsylvania, or Illinois.

Many people confuse the national forests with the national parks, but there is a great difference. The national parks preserve natural wonders for all time to come; they are like huge museums. No one is allowed to cut down trees, hunt wild game, or remove anything from the parks.

In the national forests, use is the prime consideration. In 1960, Congress passed the Multiple Use–Sustained Yield Act, which strengthens and broadens the Organic Act. Sustained yield means that a forest's "crops" are "harvested" without harming its ability to produce more crops. Multiple use means the management of all the resources of the national forests "for the greatest good of the greatest number of people."

Multiple use has five big branches: Watershed, timber, recreation, wildlife, and grazing. In addition, many widely different uses are made of the forests under "special-use permits." The Forest Service tries to manage the forests so that one use does not damage another but, instead, fits in with and even benefits the other uses.

Most of the uses of the national forest are paid for by the users, and they bring in about $220 million a year. What becomes of this money? Ten percent of it is kept for the forest where it was earned, for road-building and maintenance. Twenty-five percent goes to the counties in that forest, for county roads and schools. The remainder goes into the United States Treasury, for use as appropriated by Congress. More often than not, it is appropriated for development of the forests, and so is a self-maintaining fund for their care and improvement.

Visitors are welcome on the forests, and so we decided to visit and find out what was happening there. We hitched a little camper-trailer behind our car and took off, to travel many thousands of miles before we reached home again. We camped in national-forest campgrounds and talked to foresters on duty there, and to other campers. We visited district rangers and regional foresters, and they took us to see many exciting areas and activities on their forests.

Among other things, we learned to say *"on* the forest"; you never hear a forester say *"in* the forest."

We have tried to report some of what is going on in every field of activity. Often we have described in detail a typical example of what is happening, and have left it to the reader to realize that this happens on many other national forests, too.

Above everything, our happiest report of what we saw and did and learned is that, in truth, "forests are for people."

CONTENTS

THE NATION

Chapter 1

WHAT IS A FOREST?

We drove through the Mount Hood National Forest in Oregon, on a wide, paved highway up the shoulder of a snow-capped mountain, where towering Douglas-firs and alpine firs bank the roadsides. Close together they grow, their branches crowding each other and reaching toward the sky, their tops brown with cones. Beyond the highway, they cover the soaring mountains with a thick, surging mantle of green, reaching to the white of snow.

We walked beneath the trees, on ground soft and spongy with a thick carpet of twigs and needles. Some of the trees were so big we could not reach around them—both of us together could not reach around them.

This is a forest.

In Utah, we drove for many winding miles on the Wasatch National Forest, again on a paved highway, and saw great vistas of ponderosa pines and Douglas-firs, broken often with lush, green mountain meadows where sheep and cattle were grazing. At 9,000 to 10,000 feet, we were in the "high country" of the Wasatch Mountains. We stopped often—at a wide over-look to see the country, at a campground to wade in a sparkling mountain creek, at a nature trail to see, closeup, what grew there.

Miles and miles of the Blue Ridge Parkway in Virginia and North Carolina gave us old mountains covered with oak and sweetgum, hickory and ash—gave us masses of blossoming moun-

Douglas-fir is the number-one tree of western forests.

1

tain laurel, azaleas, and rhododendron, painting the mountain-sides with pink and rose and flame.

These, too, are forests.

In a canoe, we slipped across the sparkling waters of deep, deep lakes in Minnesota, surrounded by north woods of pine and spruce, maple and beech. In a canoe again, we floated down a wide river in Florida, where longleaf pines and live oaks were draped with Spanish moss, and palm trees and lush tropical undergrowth crowded close against the river. In a power boat, we swept across the giant ninety-mile lake of Flaming Gorge, in Utah; in a flat-bottomed boat we sampled the famous float trips of Missouri and Arkansas.

Wherever we went, we asked ourselves, "What is a forest?" We found almost as many answers as we did forests.

We camped beneath man-planted loblolly pines in Louisiana and went swimming in a lake made warm as toast by southern sun. We camped high on a flat-topped mountain in Colorado, where pine grosbeaks and stellar jays of flashing blue came

A young red fox "hides" be-hind a rock to observe an early morning hiker in a forest.

down from the firs and spruces to the ground beside our trailer. We picnicked under pinyons and junipers where camp-robbers came to our table and sat on the edge of our frying pan.

There were moose in Minnesota, and again in Wyoming; bighorn sheep in Colorado and Montana; rare trumpeter swans in Wyoming, scaled quail in Texas, deer and raccoons from East to West. In Michigan a black bear crossed the road just ahead of our car—and one just like him crossed ahead of us in Idaho.

We saw stalactite caverns, Indian mounds and Indian ruins, tidal pools and lava flows, landslides and the devastation left by floods.

All of these are things of the forest.

THE CONIFERS

We learned that to know what a forest is, you need to know what kind of trees grow in it, and how they grow. We gradually became aware that the Douglas-fir is queen of the western forests. These magnificent trees make up a large part of the forests all the way west from the east slopes of the Rocky Mountains to the Pacific, all the way north from Mexico deep into Canada. They are the number-one tree of America's lumber industry. Douglas-firs grow taller than 300 feet—taller than a thirty-story building and almost as tall as the famous redwoods; they can be ten feet thick, or more.

These are the sizes they have reached on the Pacific Coast, where the soil is rich and the rainfall may be more than 150 inches a year—and where the larger trees may be from 400 to 1,000 years old. You are much more likely, even near the Pacific, to see Douglas-firs perhaps 200 years old, 150 feet tall, more or less, and three to six feet thick. Inland through the mountain states, where altitudes soar and rainfall may lessen to twenty inches, the trees are still smaller. That they grow at all,

Douglas-fir cones hang down from the tips of the branchlets, and are "whiskered."

through this wide range of soil and climate conditions, is not much less than a miracle.

Douglas-firs grow mixed in with other trees—spruce, fir, pine, hemlock—up the shoulders of mountains, down the sides of canyons, across the floors and up the flanks of valleys and meadows. They grow in pure stands of Douglas-firs, where foresters have thinned and released them to give them every advantage. They grow over countless acres of wilderness, where saw and axe have never been put to them. *They grow*—and the forests are tremendously richer because of them.

It is strange that this champion is also a mystery. No one knows exactly what kind of tree it is. It has been called fir, spruce, hemlock, pine—but it is none of these. It seems to be a "kind" all its own. It looks much like the firs, but the cones of all the firs stand upright on the branches. Moreover, fir cones usually disintegrate on the branch after they have opened. In contrast, Douglas-fir cones hang down from the branches, and they stay intact until they fall. And they have something that sets them apart from all the others, something that marks any tree they come from as a Douglas-fir. They are "whiskered." A delicate, three-pointed bract extends from under each scale on the cone, giving it a feather-studded appearance.

The Douglas-fir is named for one of the men who discovered it, David Douglas, and is affectionately nicknamed "Doug-fir" by the foresters. Because it is not really a fir, the name is usually written with a hyphen, or even as one word—Douglasfir.

Douglas-fir forests reseed themselves easily. The trees produce an abundance of seeds every two to seven years, and the seeds scatter widely beneath the trees and germinate easily.

Second tree of the West is the fine, straight ponderosa pine, long called western yellow pine. Ponderosas grow in every western state, including North and South Dakota and Nebraska. Like the Douglas-fir, they can grow at high altitudes—up to 12,000 feet—and at sea level; in dry climate and wet; in the cold of the northern Rockies and the heat of the Southwest.

Foresters say that this tree can claim the longest continuous stand of timber in the world—one in the Southwest that starts on the national forests of New Mexico, rides west and north through Arizona, and continues north through Utah to Wyoming. In much of this vast spread, especially in New Mexico and Arizona, more than four fifths of all the trees are ponderosa pines. Yet 65 percent of all ponderosa pines grow in Washington, Oregon, and California. The total stand is greater than that of any other kind of pine in North America, and is second only to the Douglas-fir.

Ponderosas are slow-growing but can reach tremendous size. Full-grown trees often are more than 200 feet tall and five to

Ponderosa pines can grow at high altitudes— up to twelve thousand feet—and at sea level; in dry climate and wet; in the cold of the northern Rockies and the heat of the Southwest. This one is a Pacific Coast tree, where growing conditions are at their best.

eight feet thick—but "full-grown" may mean that they are close to 500 years old.

The tree grows straight and well-rooted, in many different kinds of soil. This is a long-needled pine, with needles up to eleven inches. It reseeds itself easily, from an abundance of big cones. The seeds scatter widely, drifting in the air on "wings," and the young seedlings are hardy and fast-growing.

Many other trees help make up the western forests. Lodgepole pines grow through wide areas in the Rocky Mountains, and in Alaska, Washington, Oregon, and California. These are slim, fast-growing trees that stand close together, often where fire has previously destroyed the forest. Lodgepole cones ripen every second year in big clusters that hold a wealth of seeds. In some locations they may stay on the trees for years without opening. Then fire strikes, and in a lodgepole forest it is a deadly holocaust, destroying everything—everything but seeds protected by unopened cones. Heated, the cones open, and so the area is reseeded and the lodgepoles spring up again. Without competition from brush or other trees, an even denser stand of lodgepoles is soon on its way.

Sugar pines grow mostly in the mountains of California, but spread northward far into Oregon. They are the largest of all our pines. Trees 250 feet tall and eighteen feet thick have been reported, but most of these big ones have long since been turned into lumber. The cones of sugar pines, too, are enormous, often nearly two feet long. Jeffrey pine—a tree very similar to the ponderosa—is common in California forests. And the magnificent western white pine grows throughout the mountain forests of the Pacific Coast states and Montana and Idaho, but has been tragically diminished by blister rust.

Firs, spruces, and hemlocks all play their parts in western forests. White fir grows extensively in California and is likely to be seen in almost any western state. Alpine fir lifts its tall, beautifully tapered spires in many western forests. Grand fir follows the coast of northern California and Oregon and spreads over western Washington; it grows also in northern Idaho and western Montana. Noble fir grows in the high mountain forests of Oregon and Washington, red fir in those of California and southwest Oregon. How do you recognize a fir? Look for heavy, upright, egg-shaped cones that are going to pieces while still on the branches. If you find upright, disintegrating cones on a tree, it is a fir.

Blue spruce, Sitka spruce, Engelmann spruce—these are words often on the lips of westerners. Nothing is so dear to the heart of a Coloradan as a blue spruce—a "silver" spruce—standing erect in a glory of new, silvery growth beside a mountain stream. Blue spruce is widespread in all the Rocky Mountain states. Engelmann spruce is even more common in these mountains and also those to the northwest. The Engelmann is hard to tell from the blue, because it, too, is blue-green and sometimes silvery. But it grows in big, pure stands that dominate everything else, while the blue is usually mixed in with other trees; and the Engelmann's mature cones are usually less than two inches long, while those of the blue may be three to four inches.

Biggest of spruces, the Sitka spruce is another giant of the Northwest. It grows in thick forests all the way up the Pacific Coast from California through the coastal forests of Alaska. White spruce and black spruce grow throughout much of Alaska's interior—in fact, throughout much of northern North America.

Important, too, to Alaskan coastal forests is western hemlock, a tree that grows also down the Pacific Coast into California, and in the mountains of the Northwest. It is readily recognized by its drooping branches; its needles are flat, rounded, and glossy, growing in flat sprays of branchlets, and its cones are tiny—often less than an inch long.

Almost anywhere in the South, four great pines are the forest trees—loblolly, slash, longleaf, and shortleaf. They are fast-growing trees, reaching lumber size in thirty to fifty years and coming to splendid maturity in seventy. Growing in the forest, the first three may be hard to tell apart. They all have long needles, with the loblolly growing to nine inches, the slash to twelve, the longleaf to fifteen. They all have large cones with sharp spines at the tips of the scales. The longleaf is likely to bunch its needles in lusher, richer growth than the others—in great, rounded cushions of green. The shortleaf has much shorter needles—three to five inches—and the cones average only about two inches. The shortleaf ranges through all the southern states and northeast into Pennsylvania and New Jersey. Loblolly and longleaf grow throughout the southern states, and slash pine grows in all the states of the "Deep South." Various other pines grow in one or more of the southern states—pond

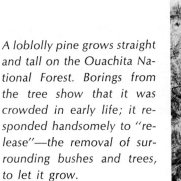

A loblolly pine grows straight and tall on the Ouachita National Forest. Borings from the tree show that it was crowded in early life; it responded handsomely to "release"—the removal of surrounding bushes and trees, to let it grow.

pine, sand pine, Virginia pine, pitch pine. But the "big four" are so important to our lumber supply that, together, they rank second only to the West's Douglas-fir.

These are some of America's most important conifers, or cone-bearing trees. There are many others. The North has its own varieties of pines and spruces. Cedars and junipers of one kind or another grow nationwide, confusing in their similarities of appearance, wood, tiny flat needles in flat sprays of branches, and fruits that look more like berries than cones. The eastern "redcedar" that grows from the plains to the Atlantic is really a juniper. The western redcedar of the Pacific Coast and northern Rockies, which sometimes reaches giant size, and the northern whitecedar of the Appalachians, New England, and the northern lake states, are true cedars; both are usually called "arborvitae." Baldcypress is a water-loving conifer growing in the southern states, but it is not an "evergreen," as it loses its needles in the fall like broad-leaved trees. The larches and tamaracks, which grow widely through the northeast quarter of the United States and in the Northwest, also shed their needles in the fall. These are the only conifers that are deciduous. The pinyons of the Southwest, the Pacific yew of coastal states and the northern Rockies—these and many others give unbelievable variety to American conifers.

THE ANCIENT ONES

Our oldest known living trees, the bristlecone pines, also are conifers; they grow only in our western mountains. The most ancient ones are on the Inyo National Forest in California's White Mountains, at 10,000 to 11,000 feet, and at Wheeler

Here is a bristlecone pine in the Ancient Bristlecone Area. It remains firmly rooted, although it seems to be quite dead. Behind it are young, living trees.

Peak in Nevada's Humboldt National Forest. In Inyo's Schulman Grove is a tree, named Pine Alpha, that is 4,300 years old; and two miles away is, appropriately, Methuselah, at 4,600 years the oldest known living tree in the world. These trees are preserved in a 28,000-acre tract, the Ancient Bristlecone Pine Area.

Bristlecones grow at such high altitudes that few other trees are found with them. Swept by high winds and battered by storms, they are twisted and bent into grotesque shapes; sometimes they are almost prostrate on the ground, but still they cling to life. Many are partly dead, with only a small vein of living tissue. They are never very tall, usually twenty-five feet or so. The name "bristlecone"comes from the sharp bristles on the scales of the three-inch-long, purplish-brown cones.

The giant sequoias are world champions in size, with trunks twenty to twenty-five feet thick and more. They grow at 4,000 to 8,500 feet on the western slopes of the Sierras, on Sierra, Stanislaus, Tahoe, and Sequoia national forests. But the largest are in national parks—Sequoia, King Canyon, and Yosemite.

The sequoias, 3,000 years old and more, are famous for their resistance to insects and disease. And they have lived through repeated fires. Their bark is so spongy and thick—often ten to twenty-four inches—that fire seldom penetrates to the living sapwood. Even then, if only a small amount of living sapwood remains, the tree will continue to bear green foliage.

The giant sequoia's cousin, the coastal redwood, third oldest living tree and probably the tallest of any, has had to fight man for its existence. But it does so better than most other conifers, because new trees will grow from sprouts on its stumps. The redwoods grow in a thirty-mile-wide belt along the Pacific Coast, from Oregon to Monterey County, California—about 500 miles. Some of these trees are 2,000 to 3,000 years old and 300 feet tall or more; the tallest is 364 feet.

Redwood lumber—strong, light, beautiful, and almost impervious to insects and weather—is highly desirable for building. Thus, many of these magnificent trees have fallen to the lumberman's saw. However, a number of groves are being protected in state parks and in a recently established Redwood National Park.

THE HARDWOODS

The northern forests of our country sweep through the Appalachian Mountains to northern Maine, and across Michigan, Wisconsin, and Minnesota. These are our "North Woods." They contain conifers in plenty—red, jack, and eastern white pine; black, white, and red spruce; eastern hemlock. But here the conifers are dominated by the hardwoods—broad-leaved trees that lose their leaves in the fall. Maple, beech, and birch grow together over great areas of these vast forests, aspen and birch in others.

Many of the hardwoods really have hard wood; for example, the rock maple and the many kinds of oaks. But some have wood softer than pine, among them the cottonwoods, aspens, and other poplars, and the tuliptree, which is often called "yellow poplar" because of its soft wood. Still, because they have broad leaves and lose their leaves in the fall, the forester includes them as "hardwoods."

One or several or many of the hardwoods grow in most of our states, but the great hardwood forests are in the central part of the country, reaching from Canada to the central South. The Chattahoochee National Forest in Georgia and the Delta in Mississippi are hardwood forests; so are the string of national forests in the Appalachian Mountains in North Carolina, West Virginia, and Pennsylvania; so are all those of the Middle West.

Hardwoods have a great variety of flowers and seeds. Most of the flowers are interesting and some are spectacular; some of the seeds are edible nuts, offering food to man as well as to wild-

A hardwood forest, on the Monongahela. Most of the large trees here are sugar maples; the one in the foreground, just at the right of center, is a red oak.

life. In autumn the hardwoods spread vistas of color—red and yellow, orange and flame—as oaks and maples and many others change color before they drop their leaves. People flock to the forests then as at no other time, "to see the colors."

Oaks and maples—several different kinds of both—are "first" trees in the hardwood forests. The white oak comes near to being the Douglas-fir of hardwoods; it is a massive, beautiful tree, three to four feet in diameter, that grows in thick stands throughout its vast range. Black oak is its close second, and northern red is another among many, all of them yielding hard, strong, durable wood that is invaluable in heavy construction and beautiful in flooring and furniture.

The sugar maple—or "hard" or "rock" maple—grows even farther northward than the white oak. Its cherished wood is used for floors, fine furniture, and choice wooden objects of all kinds. Red maple is second to it, ranging southward all the way to the Gulf of Mexico and the tip of Florida.

Many others are part of the hardwood story—birch and white ash, hickory and beech and basswood, sweetgum and blackgum (tupelo), black cherry and black walnut—all supplying wood in great variety for fine uses. The American elm was once one of them, a standout in beauty and usefulness of both tree and wood, but it is being wiped out by the Dutch elm disease. The American chestnut has disappeared because of chestnut blight.

The eastern cottonwood grows widely throughout the eastern half of the country, and where it stops, other varieties of cottonwood continue in many states all the way to the Pacific. This is a tree planted widely on the plains, where its spreading roots can be depended upon to find water; it grows along many western rivers where there are no other trees. Closely akin to it is the famous quaking aspen—both are poplars. In summer the quakies' slim silver trunks stand in dense ranks against the green of conifers, their leaves, a lighter green, trembling in the slightest breeze. By mid-fall, green has changed to purest gold and warm peach, and they paint the mountainsides with this glowing color, changing every forest road to a tunnel of gold. Look for them east of the Mississippi in the far North, and in almost any mountain forest of the West.

WHAT ELSE MAKES A FOREST?

Trees make the forest, that's certain; but other things help make it, too. What of the undergrowth in a forest—the smaller plants that give shelter and food to many kinds of animals? Some forests have little or no undergrowth. The pines and spruces of the North, the lodgepole pines, grow so close to-

By mid-fall, the green of the quakies has changed to purest gold and warm peach, and they paint the mountainsides with glowing color and change forest roads to tunnels of gold.

gether and make such dense shade that few plants grow beneath them. In fact, almost any mature conifer forest, untouched by fire or disease or logging, will be a dense forest of tall, clean trunks and high treetops that overlap in a thick canopy, shutting out most of the day's sunshine. Very little grows on the needle-blanketed floor of such a forest.

Yet the ponderosa pine forest is nearly always rather open. The trees do not like shade, and they have far-reaching root systems. So they set up strong competition for light and water, and the younger, weaker trees die out, leaving a self-thinned forest. Here, in open areas and to a lesser degree under the trees, there is an undergrowth of smaller trees and bushes, of vines, wild flowers, grasses, ferns, mosses, mushrooms. These may grow lush in the moist Pacific Coast forests, or may be scattered and sparse in the drier Rocky Mountains.

Whether a forest is open may depend upon whether it is a natural forest or one that man has thinned or planted. In the South, pines stand carefully spaced in orderly rows—great plantations of them. Yet there is not much underbrush, because man gets rid of it to allow the trees their best chance for growth.

Hardwood forests are likely to have more undergrowth than the conifers. More light comes through their canopies, especially in the spring. So you may find under the hardwoods a dense tangle of bushes and vines and a wealth of ground hugging plants. Dogwood and shad paint white ghosts in the spring with their blossoms, and witch hazel throws out a delicate tracery of gold in the fall. Woodbine climbs high into the trees, catbriar is everywhere. Anemones and trillium, violets and marsh marigolds throw a colorful pattern over the deeply leaf-strewn forest floor.

The vegetation in a forest dictates the kinds of animals that live in it. Deer live where there are browse plants—plants ranging from low-growing bushes and ground cover to willows and alders and quakies. Squirrels live where there are the seeds of conifers, the acorns of oaks, the nuts of butternut and hickory. Raccoons, foxes, bobcats, birds of many kinds live where the forest gives them food and shelter.

The animals themselves often determine the nature of a forest. Too many deer can eat all the undergrowth—all the ground cover and bushes, every branch they can reach. Squirrels, birds, and mice can eat so many seeds that the forest cannot reseed itself. Beavers can build a dam and make a lake in a forest.

Climate and altitude have great influence on the nature of the forest. Along the Pacific Coast, rain forests grow from sea level up the wet western slopes of the mountains. Here some of the giants of the forests reach their greatest sizes—Sitka spruce, Douglas-fir, western redcedar, western hemlock. Rain-forest undergrowth is lush with bushes, vines, tall ferns, and mosses. Similarly, tropical forests in Florida and along the southern coast of Texas are the product of warmth and moisture.

In great contrast to these are the thousands of acres of high-altitude pinyon-juniper forests in the Southwest. Pinyons are small, scrubby cousins of the pines; they are makers of the famous sweet-tasting "pinyon nuts." The trees are gnarled and twisted, and they can live on dry, rocky, windy hillsides where almost nothing else grows. But some junipers are usually there, too, and there is often a ground cover of sagebrush and tough grasses.

In Arizona and New Mexico are "island" mountain ranges that rise up from the desert floor to altitudes of several thousand feet. Growing there are forests that change from typical desert plants at the mountains' feet to the conifers and other growth of high levels, reaching into the alpine zone. A good example of this kind of forest is described on pages 162-163.

FORESTS ARE MANY THINGS

To know a forest, you need to know how people are using it—and taking care of it, or are not taking care of it.

Forests are many things to many people. To millions of

These big trees, left to right, are western hemlock and Sitka spruce, growing in a rain forest, the Quinalt Natural Area of the Olympic National Forest. The dense growth in the foreground is made up of young hemlock, seeded by the older trees.

people, they are a place to have fun—a place for camping, hiking, swimming, fishing, hunting, skiing—a place to see beautiful and interesting American country. To millions, although the people themselves may be only dimly aware of it, forests are the source of the water they use every day. To the lumbermen— the people who make their living by buying timber, sawing it into lumber, and selling it—forests are where the timber grows. To the rancher or farmer, the forest is a place of grass, where he can pasture his sheep or cattle. To the miner, it is a treasure-house of underground riches, and often the trees are more a nuisance than an asset.

To people who enjoy watching animals and learning about them, forests are a place to see many kinds of animals in their natural surroundings. To foresters, a forest is like a garden or a farm or a ranch—something to be tended, to be kept beautiful, to be managed to raise a crop; something to be protected from fire and insects and disease.

Forests are many things. What is a forest to you?

Chapter 2

MAKING RAINDROPS WALK

Water runs downhill.

That is a simple statement of a fact that everyone probably learns by the time he has finished the first grade. The fact is simple—but its importance is tremendous.

We keep on meeting it, again and again and again. Hardly a day passes that we do not experience it in some way. Water runs down through a drain in the sink, and joins sewer water, also running down, and we have a means of disposing of sewage. Water soaks down through the soil and reaches the roots of plants, and we have trees and grass and vegetables and wheat. There are many other ways in which water running down affects the lives of people.

Because water runs downhill, we have such a thing on the land as a "watershed." Water overflows from springs and lakes, rain falls and snow melts; and so we have rivulets and creeks and rivers, all flowing down, down, down.

Since the "down" of our land is usually in one general direction in any given area, the streams tend to flow toward each other. Little streams combine to make big streams, and eventually they flow into one big stream—the deepest "down" of the area. The area itself is thus a "watershed" or a "drainage." It can be big or little, long or short. The watershed of the Colo-

This water, near the source of the Uncompahgre River in western Colorado, is used over and over before it reaches the mouth of the Colorado River.

rado River extends from Colorado's mountains through Utah, Arizona, Nevada, and California; hundreds of smaller watersheds contribute to it. The watershed of the St. Marys River in Florida is only a few miles long, starting in southern Georgia and ending in northern Florida. The watershed for the city of Portland, Oregon, is a group of springs and short mountain rivulets that feed a giant lake.

THE BULL RUN WATERSHED

Almost every city uses one watershed or another to get its water—water for drinking, for bathing, for washing dishes, for watering the lawn—for all the things where water is necessary. Naturally, keeping that water pure is important. To keep its water from being polluted and from being used for other purposes, Portland long ago secured a "closed" watershed on U.S. Forest land; in 1917 the United States Congress set aside the Bull Run Watershed on Mount Hood National Forest for Portland's water.

The Bull Run Watershed is a long oblong whose western end is thirty miles east of Portland. The oblong runs eastward for another thirty miles, enclosing the Bull Run River and Bull Run Lake. The river starts at Bull Run Lake, curves northward for several miles, and then south again. Near the west end of the oblong, two big dams across the river make Reservoirs Number One and Two.

Towering, snow-capped Mount Hood is a striking background for this area of beautiful forests and sparkling blue lakes. But the mountain is not a major part of the Bull Run Watershed. Bull Run's water, lake and river, comes from underground springs and runoff from nearer mountainsides.

Bull Run Lake, 300 feet deep, has two outlets, both underground. One emerges after a short distance and makes the river. The other? Who knows? Dye has been put in the water to trace it, but the lake keeps its secret. The course and destination of the second outlet is a mystery.

This whole area, about 300 square miles, is almost entirely national forest land. It has been made the very acme of good watershed management. From the several thousand gallons of water held by the original 1916 reservoir, the demands of Portland have grown, and grown, and grown. But the supply has kept pace. Today Reservoir Number One holds eight billion gallons of water and Reservoir Two, ten billion—water that is unusually pure. It shoots down to Portland through huge conduits at the rate of 225 million gallons a day.

At Head Works, near the reservoirs, all sediment and leaf trash are removed just before the water drops into the conduits. And here a slight amount of chlorine is added to guard against natural pollution. A laboratory checks the quality of the water, carefully noting the amount of silt and trash in it, the temperature, and the amount of plankton—the accumulated one-celled plants and animals that are present in almost any water. If the quality of the water changes in any way, Head Works can make corrections to insure its purity.

Why is this water more pure to begin with than most open water? Because Bull Run is a closed reserve. There is one road in, and a gatekeeper stops anyone who is not there officially. No multiple use here—no fishing or hunting or camping or picnicking or hiking or skiing; no mining or grazing.

But there is one other important harvest on this watershed forest. By careful experimentation, the Forest Service proved that timber could be cut without harming the watershed—would, in fact, improve it. So now, through cooperation between the city of Portland and the Forest Service, forty to fifty million feet of lumber are harvested from the watershed every year.

Some important safeguards protect the watershed from damage by logging. First, all roads are very carefully controlled

Bull Run Lake, three hundred feet deep, has two outlets, both underground. One emerges after a short distance and makes the river. The other? Who knows? Dye has been put in the water to trace it, but the lake keeps its secret. The course and destination of the second outlet is a mystery.

and managed. Although there is just one road into the watershed, there is a network of more than 500 miles of roads inside its fence. These are small roads, carefully laid out to avoid erosion problems, that today's jeeps can travel without trouble.

Another safeguard is the care used in selecting the area where trees are to be cut. Some thirty-five or forty acres at a time are cut, taking all the trees, and so the area chosen must be one that is mostly mature trees. It must be so situated, and the operation so timed, that damage from erosion from heavy rainfall will be

at a minimum. There must be time for some ground cover to grow again, before the rainy season.

Still another important protection is given the surrounding forest. Usually, trucks do not go up the mountainside to the cutover area. Instead, a "yard" or "landing" is set up near a road, and the area is "cable logged." The cable, 600 feet to a half-mile long, runs to the area and carries logs through the air to trucks at the landing. Thus, high ridges and vulnerable tracts are harvested without damage by travel across them.

These huge logs were carried by cable from a heavily forested area on Bull Run Watershed.

Using these modern methods, the Forest Service has shown that timber can be harvested without seriously disturbing the soil and so causing erosion. The logging company is required to clean up both the cutover area and the landing, and leave them is such condition that they can be replanted with seedlings. So a young, vigorous stand of trees is always coming on, improving the watershed and keeping it alive.

WATERSHEDS FROM COAST TO COAST

In the beginning, national forests were mostly in the West. But swift growth of the nation, with expanding population and growing industry, was taking place east of the Mississippi.

In the East, the South, the Middle West, cutting for lumber and clearing for farming had taken off much of the watershed forest and left the land open to flooding and erosion. It soon became apparent that something had to be done about the watersheds. Cities did it, by buying up surrounding lands. The Forest Service did it, by buying, too, under a new law, the Weeks Law. Both Forest Service and cities were interested primarily in water. To save water, they reforested watersheds.

Today, in the northeast quarter of America, there are more than 400 city-owned watersheds—watersheds that are the property of cities such as Boston, Hartford, Newark, and many others. They hold much more than a million acres of forests and provide water for more than fifty million people. More vast forested acreages are owned by states and water associations, and these, too, bring water to hundreds and hundreds of communities.

Other hundreds in this eastern half of America are dependent on the watersheds of the national forests—forests such as the White Mountain in New Hampshire and Maine, the Allegheny in Pennsylvania, the Monongahela in West Virginia, the forests of North Carolina and Tennessee and Kentucky, of Missouri and Arkansas.

These are forests whose reason for being is the security of watersheds—their replanting, rebuilding, and continued protection. In Arkansas alone there are nearly three-and-a-half million acres within Forest Service boundaries, mostly in the Ouachita and Ozark forests, and mostly purchased to rebuild watersheds. Rivers such as the Little Missouri and the Ouachita rise in the forests and carry water down from them to the cities of Little Rock, Fort Smith, and many others, large and small.

The western half of America adds vast acreages to the lands of watershed importance. Many are somewhat like Bull Run and Portland. Water goes to Denver, Colorado, from the watersheds on the Arapaho and Pike national forests; to Tacoma, Washington, from a 147,000-acre watershed on the Snoqualmie.

Even in the West, many cities own their watersheds; Seattle

Whether you dip it from a high mountain stream or take it from the tap in your kitchen, water is probably the most precious resource of the national forests.

owns a whopping 66,000 acres on the Cedar River. But the chances are, if you live anywhere from the Rocky Mountains west, at least some of the water you use every day comes from a national forest watershed. In California, twelve million people get their domestic water from national forests, and two thirds of irrigation water comes from them. In the Intermountain Region, three fourths of all water used comes from national forest watersheds.

How strict is protection of watersheds? Foresters estimate that 92 percent have at least two other uses—logging, grazing, mining, fishing, hunting, or camping. Grazing is usually not allowed on critical watersheds, since it may contribute both to pollution and to erosion. Logging is often allowed, but always under careful management. People come and go on almost all watersheds.

Foresters try to meet the heavy demands of other uses of the forest. But if the watershed is endangered, other uses are likely to be limited or closed entirely for a time. The safety of the water comes first. If the watershed dies, everything dies.

SPECIAL PROTECTION

How do you protect millions of acres of watersheds? How do you restore so much as an acre, after its trees and its soil have gone down the drain? Good questions, these, when water pollution and water shortages are multiplying wherever population is increasing. And the national forests have, in action, some good answers.

It is easier to prevent erosion than to cure it. So watersheds are kept under close watch for threat of erosion—for loss of grass on a mountain shoulder, or failure of a cutover or burned area to come back, or, especially, for the telltale sign of many little gullies cutting their way down to a larger one.

There the foresters go to work. They plow contour furrows

around the face of a slope, so that water can no longer run straight down it, but will be slowed up and will soak into the ground. They plant a contoured hillside or a cutover or burned area with grass, shrubbery, and small trees, so that the soil will have a protecting, growing cover as well as the springy, lively topsoil that results from the dropping of needles, leaves, and other litter. And in the gullies they build check dams of rocks and logs, to slow down the flow of water and silt and gradually fill the gullies.

In the words of a famous conservationist, foresters work to "make the raindrops walk instead of run upon the land."

Many times in America's history, prevention has not come in time, and terrifying, destroying floods have swept down from sick watersheds to bury towns and farms in water and mud. This happened again and again in Utah—in Davis County south of Ogden, and southward through what is now the Manti-LaSal National Forest. In the way of the West, towns here are often at the mouths of canyons and big gulches, the watersheds

Left to themselves, small gullies swiftly grow into big ones, ruining great acreages of farm and forest lands.

sweeping high and wide above them. Gradually, by fire and by grazing, vegetation on the sidehills was killed out, the soil left bare. Then came heavy rains, and floods rushed down on the towns below. Their streets were filled with mud and rocks to the size of huge boulders; the neighboring farms were covered with a thick, smothering layer of silt.

From these tragedies came a new development. The Forest Service had an experimental watershed in Davis County, in the northern part of Wasatch National Forest, where it was pioneering the use of contouring to prevent erosion. So foresters contoured one hillside after another that had been denuded and gouged by the floods—contoured and planted, contoured and planted. They built gully plugs and check dams—and planted. In a year or two, slopes that had been completely bare were covered again with healthy grass and bushes, and foresters had proved that a ruined watershed could be healed.

Similar things were happening all over the country. The watershed above Boise, Idaho, washed out and the city was flooded with water and mud. In Colorado, in Utah, in California, the story was repeated. A disastrous fire on the watershed above Deadwood, South Dakota, stripped the vegetation and left the land exposed to erosion. But here was a happier ending. Foresters, forewarned, contoured the hillsides and replanted them. A thick growth of new vegetation covered the burned-over watershed before heavy rains came—and Deadwood had no disastrous flood.

Often, rebuilding a watershed is not done just by the Forest Service, but by many different agencies working together. A shining example of what can be done in this way is the Yazoo-Little Tallahatchie Flood Prevention Project in northern Mississippi. This was once a beautiful area of forests, meadows, and streams—but the forests were cleared and the land was left to erode. Over 100 million tons of sand and sediment were washed

Check dams catch the silt and slow up the flow of water.

out of the hills each year, down into the streams and valleys. Great gullies eroded the meadows and fields, where the soil was lost at a rate of 300 tons per acre, every year. Land became worthless, and the people of this great area were impoverished.

But the people were still able to pull themselves together and move against destruction. They enlisted the Forest Service, the Soil Conservation Service, the conservation forces of Mississippi, and they formed committees among themselves. All together, they worked to fill the gullies and to replant them and the hillsides with grass, bushes, and trees. Today, this area is again a forested watershed, its land valuable, beautiful to look at, and a protector of water.

Contouring the slopes, planting, checking and damming the gullies—these are the foresters' first-line weapons against erosion. More than anything else, foresters plant, plant, plant. They agree that in the struggle against erosion, nothing is so valuable as a blanket of vegetation over the soil. Foresters have achieved it—are achieving it—over hundreds of thousands of acres. But a big part of the job still looms ahead. In the Intermountain Region, which includes Utah, 125,000 critical acres have been reclaimed and protected; but 860,000 acres remain to be worked. In the Rio Grande Basin of Colorado and New Mexico, in California, in most of America, much erosion-threatened watershed land has been protected—about 500,000 acres. But on three-and-a-half million acres, this work is still to be done. The Forest Service hopes to gain "reasonable control" of those acres in the next ten years. But a great deal depends on how much money they have for the job, and on the amount of new damage from storms, flood, and fire.

INCREASING THE WATER CROP

Protection is not the whole story. Today, when you talk to a forester about watersheds, he uses such words as "yield," "harvest," "crop." Water is a crop, then? Definitely. Moreover, it is a crop that can be increased in certain proven ways.

We recognize that in any downpour, much water soaks into the ground, and much of that is absorbed by the roots of trees and other plants. From the roots it travels through stems into leaves, where it is "breathed" or transpired into the air as vapor. All this—about 35 percent of total rainfall—is lost to us as water, until it again becomes part of rainfall or snowfall.

The watershed management program has proved that sagebrush transpires less water than trees, and that grass uses less than sagebrush. So stream flow can be substantially raised by converting trees and brush to grass.

In the western states, where rainfall is often less than twenty inches in a year—twelve in Arizona, eight in Nevada—anything that can increase man's water supply is especially important. Here dramatic results are indicating great possibilities for increasing water from the watersheds by changing the kind of vegetation. In experiments in California, Arizona, and New Mexico, brush has been pulled out and grass planted; various native plants that use a great deal of water are being replaced by others that use much less. Stream flow in these experiments has consistently increased.

Many times the change of plant cover is only temporary. A forty-acre area, say, is selected where the "lie" and a scarcity of ground cover will not subject it to erosion. The trees are clear cut, carefully, so as not to disturb the ground around them. The ground cover may be sufficient, or grasses may be planted; and seedlings are planted to start a new stand of trees. For fifteen to twenty years, there is less use of water in this area by plants —until, as a forester puts it, the vegetation has grown enough "to get back to pumping it out again." By that time, other areas have been clear cut, and so the saving of water has become an annual process and may be increased, without decreasing the production of timber.

What becomes of the water so saved, the water that plants don't use? Some of it drains off on underground layers of rock, into streams and springs and lakes. Some soaks down all the way to the water table, and raises it, so that it replenishes streams, lakes, springs, and wells. In either case, there is more water that can be harvested by man for his fields and his cities.

Especially desirable is an increase of water during the "low-flow" season. In many parts of America, spring and early summer bring heavy rain and melting snow, and there is quick and heavy runoff, with drought following during summer and autumn.

The Forest Service is experimenting with snowfall control in order to slow down and extend the annual runoff. They have learned how to cut timber so that snow will pile up in strategic open areas and last longer. Sometimes they put up snow fences to catch snow and hold it in huge drifts. Sometimes they cut strips in the forest to act as snow fences, where the accumulated snow will be shaded by timber.

Probably the greatest means of holding water back from fast runoff is the hundreds of dams and reservoirs all over America. Here the water of a fast-flowing river can be backed up and held in a man-made lake, and released gradually as it is needed by communities and farmers downstream.

Most of the dams are built not by the Forest Service but by the U.S. Bureau of Reclamation or the Corps of Engineers of the U.S. Army. But a heavy responsibility for the reservoirs rests with the Forest Service. For example, if silt washes into a reservoir and gradually fills it, its capacity to store water will be greatly reduced. The foresters' job is to hold the silt on the watersheds, where it belongs.

A farm pond and loblollies replace eroded acres in Yazoo–Little Tallahatchie flood-control project.

As the work of experimenting with watersheds went forward, the Forest Service developed a system of "barometer" watersheds. There are twenty-three of them, in eighteen states; most recently established is one in Alaska, on the Tongass National Forest. They are scattered over the country in order to cover every kind of land and climate that we have, and especially to cover the "problem" lands.

Barometer watersheds range from about 50,000 to 150,000 acres. They put into practice the information coming from the many experiments; and they, too, continue to experiment and assemble information. Scientists work year-round with every modern instrument and device they can find or invent. In all kinds of weather, on all kinds of land, with all kinds of trees and ground plants, they study and record rainfall, runoff, silt-

Sometimes strips are cut in the forest to act as snow fences, where accumulated snow will be shaded by timber.

ing; the effects and costs of water-yield improvement measures; the effects on the watersheds of lumbering, wildlife, recreation. These watersheds are centers for distributing information about every region, to all those interested—to national and state and county forests, to towns and cities, to private landowners.

Clearly, watershed management is a complex program that spreads all over the country. And the Forest Service is not alone in it. Their activities coincide and cooperate with those of many other agencies. The U. S. Soil Conservation Service works closely with the Forest Service, and so do the Bureau of Reclamation, the Army Corps of Engineers, and the National Water Resources Board. Also cooperating are many regional associations of various kinds, such as the Pacific Northwest River Basins Commission. And the Forest Service gives important help to many large-scale water conservation projects—regional studies like that for the Columbia-North Pacific and the Colorado River Storage Project.

In watershed management, regardless of agency, the guiding spirit is "Manage for the greatest good to the most people." As we stood at the edge of Bull Run Lake in that immaculate watershed, reflecting beautiful, snow-capped Mount Hood and surrounded by magnificent pine and Douglas-fir forest, we felt a touch of sadness that the public is shut out of this lovely spot. But we remembered the millions of acres where the public is welcome, many of them just as lovely, and we cannot quarrel with a policy that guarantees clean water to millions of people.

Chapter 3

TIMBER-R-R-R!

This year and every year, a crop worth more than $300 million is being harvested on your property. This idea may take some getting used to, because you don't hear much about the harvesting, and you may not realize that you own this valuable property. But own it you do, you and all the other citizens of the United States. And it is becoming increasingly valuable with every passing year.

In the United States there are more than 760 million acres of forested lands. About 510 million of these are "commercial" forests—those with timber that can be turned into lumber. About 97 million acres of "commercial" forests are in the national forests. This is a little less than one fifth of all the commercial forests, yet from them comes almost one third of the wood used in the United States.

Nationwide, you see the logs coming out of the forests, loaded on trucks, stacked high on railroad cars, floated in great rafts on quiet rivers, lakes, and harbors—all on their way to bustling sawmills to make our lumber. A huge lion's share of them comes from the West—fir and pine, spruce, hemlock, redwood. But pine comes from the South, too, in large quantities, and from the North; and hardwoods come from eastern and central states.

Timber is the biggest crop of the national forest, as measured in dollars. It accounts for about 94 percent of the total receipts.

A power saw cuts swiftly through a giant Sitka spruce, on a national forest in Alaska.

"Saw timber" is by far the biggest part of that. Saw timber is made up of trees large enough, straight enough, and solid enough so that boards can be sawed from them. Here is the source of the boards and beams in your house, of all the boards and planks and beams of all structures that use wood in their framework or sheathing or finishing. Remembering that today two homes are being built for every one built ten years ago, and that forecasts see three being built ten years from now, it is not hard to understand that the demand for saw timber is doubling and doubling again. Add to that the skyrocketing demand for "round" timber—logs four to ten inches in diameter that go into pulp for paper, and into many other wood products.

So what is happening to the national forests, where much of this wood is being produced—to your property? Are they being denuded, to keep up with the demand?

TAKING OUT THE TREES

Logging methods in all forests have changed since the days when man tromped over the land, cutting down the trees for wood, burning what he didn't want at the moment. Most commercial forests are logged today by practices that promote the growth of new trees to replace the old. This is basic policy in the management of national forests.

The Forest Service itself does no logging. It sells the standing timber to commercial companies, but it strictly regulates the logging methods to be used.

First, the land itself is considered. Land on which logging is done can be left torn-up and ravaged. If immense trees are recklessly felled and dragged by tractor or "skidded" downhill to a truck—if the truck itself is on a road planned only to get the logs out—the land and the forest can be fatally damaged.

How, then, is logging carried on? Does a lone man climb the tree and top it? Does a crew then cut through the base with axe

Logging trucks line up at a Forest Service checking station on Willamette National Forest, Oregon. Some of the logs are so large that three of them make a load for one truck.

and saw, arduously, sometimes taking hours for it? Does the cry of "Timber-r-r-r!" go ringing through the forest as each tree falls?

This was a pattern once followed fairly widely in all forests. But things have been happening to logging equipment. It has become power equipment. And one of the most important things that foresters are doing today is finding out how it can best be used.

Here they meet not just one set of problems but many. This is a big land, and it contains many different kinds of country— low, flat lands, often marshy; high, rugged mountains with cliffs and steep mountain shoulders. The machinery that might be practical and easy to use on flat land is likely to be altogether unusable on a mountainside.

How do they log a mountainside today? By skidding the logs down it? Yes, if the hillside is not too steep. "Skid trails" are used, where the logs are pulled by tractor to a landing and then loaded onto trucks. The location of skid trails is of great importance and must meet with Forest Service approval. To avoid having a skid trail become a roaring sluice with every rain, drainage ways are installed by the logging company to divert water. These drainage ways are part of every timber sale contract in the mountains, where skid trails are to be used. So are the locations of the landings.

Many mountainsides in the West are lush with marketable timber but too steep for even the most carefully controlled skid logging. Here, today's steel and power machinery are performing miracles. With the speed and grace of the man on the flying trapeze, a giant log comes winging through the air on a steel cable to the landing. The cable is strung from a tall "spar tree" in some rugged, inaccessible spot where the timber is prime. It runs to another spar tree or a steel tower at the landing, where

At the landing, logs are loaded onto the truck that will take them to a sawmill. These big "peelers" are western hemlock and Douglas-fir.

Loggers use a power saw to cut a ponderosa pine on Okanogan National Forest, Washington.

the logs are picked up by a powerful winch and loaded onto trucks. The landing is only a step or two from an improved road, which takes the trucks without difficulty to paved highways outside the forest.

Cables can be run from high places to low, or the other way around—from a hard-to-reach valley to a ridge where there is a road; they run out 600 or 800 or 1,000 feet to reach the source of the timber. Sometimes the cables are run from one ridge to another—a "skyline system"—where the cables may be 4,000 feet or longer.

Cable logging eliminates more than the skid trail hazard. Here there is no need at the timber source for the wide, heavy-duty roads that trucks require. Jeeps go in on a minimum trail, carrying cable equipment and loggers. They can go onto a watershed, for example, and cable out valuable timber without disturbing earth and surrounding young forest.

Power machinery has changed, too, the work of felling treees. Once, two men, one on each end of a long hand saw, had a big job ahead of them to cut through a good timber tree. With today's power saw, two men can fell an acre of timber in a day —and this in spite of the fact that they still have to put their trees down where they want them to fall. The fallen trees cannot cross, and they have to go in the right direction.

Lumbermen agree that the biggest cost in logging is getting the logs onto trucks and hauling them to a sawmill. And they have learned that the most destructive method of taking out logs is often the most expensive for them; a cable system may be less expensive than beating against an almost inaccessible terrain day after day. So lumbermen work along with the Forest Service to find ways that will quickly, easily, and without waste get trucks loaded with logs and on their way over a good road.

THE VALUE OF TIMBER

And a valuable load it is. That big truck you just met: It had only three giant logs aboard, yet they bulked high overhead. Do you have any notion how much this load is worth? (One out of three loads is your property, remember.) These three logs are all prime saw timber, and together they will produce somewhere near 10,000 board feet of lumber. The logger pays about $100 per thousand board feet for this kind of lumber. So he has paid you about $1,000 for this one load. Add his costs and his profit to that, and you may be looking at three logs worth close to $1,000 apiece.

They are, remember, "prime" logs—probably Douglas-fir. Foresters call them "peelers," because they are big enough to be peeled in large sheets, for expensive veneers and for plywood.

From here to pulpwood and chips, value drops sharply.

Nevertheless, a timber sale in Mount Hood National Forest in Oregon recently netted $1.5 million for twenty-six million board feet. Remember that this is one sale from only one small part of Oregon's thirteen national forests, and we begin to see something of the proportions of this tremendous national resource that you own. It is, in short, a resource that markets twelve billion board feet of lumber every year.

THE ALLOWABLE CUT

If today's figure of marketed timber is amazing, there is a still more amazing fact back of it: It represents only a small part of the total marketable timber in the national forests. In the whole Pacific Northwest Region, about five billion board feet of trees are taken out each year. Yet the annual "allowable cut" for that region of far-flung forests is less than 2 percent of trees that are as large as eleven inches in diameter.

What is an "allowable cut"? Simply the number of trees that can be cut, in a doling out that must eventually end? Or, perhaps, the number that, cut today, can be replanted tomorrow? Far from it! Either of these would result in long periods in which there would be no timber for cutting.

The procedure of "allowable cut" is much more complex and much more rewarding. It is based on the number of trees that *are coming into maturity* today or a very early tomorrow. Mature trees are taken out. Behind them must be growing trees to replace them—and soon. The time may vary from one part of the country to another, or from one forest situation to another; it takes longer for trees to grow in one kind of climate or soil than in another. But the policy is always the same. We sell timber only as fast as it is being replaced by growing, maturing trees.

In Forest Service terminology, this is "continual harvest" or "sustained yield." It is what foresters mean when they say that "the timber resource is renewable." They not only harvest the crop, but they so manage forest lands that a new crop is always coming along—is, in fact, always ready.

CLEAR CUTTING AND REPLANTING

In the past a much-favored method for selecting timber to be cut was that of marking individual trees that should be taken out —were mature, or imperfect, or were handicapping the trees around them. But taking out individual trees is often an expensive process and is often destructive to nearby trees. Moreover, in "managed" forests, trees tend to level off in age groups, and the trees of a rather large area may all become mature at about the same time. So, as the years go by, the practice of "selective cutting" becomes less and less effective.

In most forests where timber is being cut today, at least some of it is "clear cut," and a great deal of it may be. Clear cutting is the practice of selecting an acreage, probably not more than forty acres and usually somewhat less, and cutting the entire stand.

What happens, then, to the forty acres? First, the logger is required to clean up the land he has logged. He has topped his his trees and trimmed the branches from them; the resulting "slash" is a great bed of trash. Sometimes he piles it into windrows, and, when the weather is right, the Forest Service burns it. But, increasingly, the Forest Service is able to utilize the slash in ways that are still under development, or to dispose of it without burning. The soil is worked to loosen it, leaving a good seed bed covered with light forest litter.

In many forests, the forty acres will reseed themselves naturally, from seeds that fell before or during the logging. Here even

The log harvest is often brought to the sawmill by water, in rafts like this one on the St. Joe River in Idaho.

the burning helps, because some cones—jack pines, and others—will not open and release their seeds until they have been heated.

Many tracts, however, must be planted, either with seeds or with seedlings one to three years old. A million acres of trees have been planted by the Forest Service in Oregon alone, a fact that indicates the towering size of this one job. And again, today's machinery is playing almost a miracle role.

From one part of the country to another, different problems in planting must be met. On the rough and rocky land and steep slopes of many western forests, hand planting has been the rule because planting by machine was so difficult and unsatisfactory there. Machines did not get seedlings into the soil at a correct and even depth; the wheels rolled over them and ground them under. Contour planting around a sidehill, so important to prevent erosion, was impossible because the machines could not follow a slope.

But today's machine—the "Forestland Tree Planter"—is doing the job. Years went into developing it; now it can set the seedling trees, evenly spaced, on rough ground and in the circular pattern of a sidehill, and can pack them in firmly without damaging them. In a single day, it can plant 4,800 seedling trees on a rocky, steep slope. Nearly all of these trees survive.

The South, too, has its planting problems. On Ocala National Forest in Florida, for example, two trees are fine producers of saw timber—slash pine and longleaf pine. Slash pine starts easily and fast. But if it is too high above water, on the rolling hills and ridges typical of this area, it doesn't do well after the first few years; its roots don't reach enough water. Longleaf pines, on the other hand, grow beautifully on the uplands. But natural reseeding here is almost nonexistent, because there are so many squirrels that they keep the seeds cleaned up. So if the foresters want longleaf pines, they have to plant the seeds.

Planting seeds by hand is a slow and expensive process, but

Here is an animal—the porcupine—that foresters don't much like, and from which trees need to be protected. His preferred food is the bark of pine trees, and he often kills the treetops in young plantations. And he kills older trees when he girdles them to strip off the bark.

this job in an hour or less. It makes a tape that can be monitored in the helicopter, played back at any time, and used as a guide to return to that exact spot for re-examination, either from the air or from the ground.

Foresters believe there are tremendous possibilities in the uses of sensors—that they have only made a beginning in using them to protect forests all over the country. A hint of the future comes in the possible use of satellites. Just as they send television programs and weather reports back to earth, they can feed back information on timber that is being invaded by insects and disease. So, twenty years from now, you may build a house with lumber that was protected by satellite.

Every bit of this protection and more is needed to save enormous quantities of timber from the ravages of disease and insects. Much effort, publicity, and money have gone into the campaign to cut down loss of timber from fire. Foresters estimate that three times as many trees die from disease and insect-invasion as are lost by fire.

Anyone who has seen a white pine turning brown from blister rust can understand how these magnificent trees have been almost wiped out by the disease. Anyone seeing the devastation caused by mountain pine beetles in the great lodgepole pine forests of the Rockies wonders if the lodgepoles, too, will be wiped out—the only timber tree that will grow in many parts of the mountain forests. And anyone who has ever sprayed a rose bed for insects or mildew knows what a demanding, expensive, time-consuming job it is. It is an impossible job over the far reaches of growing forests, yet necessary if we are to keep our forests. Our hope to do it successfully seems to lie in such new tools as sensors, operated from the air in scanning systems that can quickly locate infected areas while they are small.

A very heartening fact is connected with all these problems. The people of the Forest Service who are developing new tools, testing them out, and patiently redeveloping them live by the slogan, "There's nothing that can't be done." And, day by day, they're proving it.

TIMBER MANAGEMENT AT WORK

All of these activities add up to "timber management," and that is far from a new idea with the Forest Service.

In the South, as recently as 1930, thousands on thousands of cutover acres were left to the mercies of fire and erosion. This land was completely unproductive, a hazard instead of an asset in the protection of water supplies—a weight around the neck of all nearby communities. The Forest Service bought it up—the only "takers"—and, painstakingly, piece by piece and tree by tree, planted it to seedlings; the planting was often done by hand. Civilian Conservation Corps crews working in the 1930's did much of the work.

Today these lands are blanketed with magnificent forests of pines that are already reaching marketable maturity, and are also protecting watersheds on which millions of people depend. In Mississippi alone, more than $45 million has been received from timber sales from national forests since reforestation. On the great Ouachita National Forest in Arkansas and Oklahoma, more than $3 million worth of wood is cut every year—shortleaf pine, white oak, red oak, and gum. These woods go into lumber, paper, posts, poles, furniture, barrel staves, veneer, and a host of "specialty" items that are made from wood.

In some of the Great Lakes states, too, vast acreages have been replanted. Michigan leads here with more than 675,000 acres—nearly one fourth of this state's national forests. Wisconsin and Minnesota each have about a quarter million acres of replanted forests. Annual income from national forest timber has increased substantially in these states since reforestation; in Michigan it is close to a million dollars.

And in North Carolina, where nearly 50,000 acres have been replanted, the annual timber cut nears the million-dollar mark.

The value of these sales is not by any means confined to the wood alone. Loggers and truck drivers and mechanics and sawmill operators live in nearby communities and pay for their living, to the tune of $25 for every dollar's worth of timber sold and cut. To the communities near the Ouachita and inside its boundaries, that means an annual income of more than $50 million. In some of the big-timber western states, this figure goes very high indeed—perhaps to $2 billion in Oregon, to $600 million in California. Without logging in the national forests, many towns might cease to prosper or even to exist.

So it is easy to understand that timber management is aimed, first and foremost, at improving the timber stand. From this direction can come more and better lumber in a tree, more good trees in an acre, and more big trees in a shorter time. All or any of these can increase the allowable cut without endangering the living forest.

Increases have, in fact, already come. In 1950, about three-and-a-half billion board feet of lumber were taken from the national forests. Today, as we have seen, their annual production is more than twelve billion. Clearly, they are already producing more than their share of the country's wood—and the dividends from good timber management are only just beginning to come in.

So in every year, the Forest Service continues to replant more than 250,000 acres, much of it with seedlings but much of it, too, with seeds. Reseeding on the ground is an old dream of the foresters—one that bypasses all the time and effort and money necessary to grow seedlings, transport them, and set them in the ground. Many times unsuccessful, direct seeding still succeeds often enough to hold out hope for future development. After especially destructive recent fires in Montana, men were getting seeds back into the ground while the ashes were still hot; the seeds sprouted and grew, and so today young forests are coming along on these burned-over lands. Seeding from the air by plane or helicopter to get quick action in inaccessible areas, has often been successful.

How do cultivation and logging affect the other uses of the forest? Is clear cutting, for example, good for the wildlife in a forest? Foresters say it is, that it makes openings where small shrubs soon start to grow and provide good forage for deer, elk, and other plant-eating animals. Foresters have come to recognize a surprising fact—that a dense, mature forest is usually not a good home for wildlife. Tall, mature trees make good timber, but they do not provide food for deer. Deer prosper in areas where there are openings in the forest that give them shrubs to eat.

What about watersheds? Does clear cutting endanger a watershed? As we have seen, certain basic safeguards are observed on a watershed; and it often profits from clear cutting by an important increase in its water crop.

The visitor's use of the forest is considered, too, even though he may be just a passerby on a paved highway through the forest. Areas next to the highways are not clear cut, because in the first year or two, a clear-cut tract may break unpleasantly into the appearance of a great green blanket of trees. If a tract to be clear cut lies in a scenic area, seen at a distance from a highway, its lines can often be shaped and blended with the surrounding forest to appear as a natural opening. Landscape architects, working for the Forest Service, do this special job of landscape preservation.

All of this adds up to a strong belief of today's forester: Good

Foresters plant seedlings to replace forests burned by the Sundance fire in Idaho.

timber management results in good management of all the forest's resources.

Even so, the strongest point in its favor is likely to be, today and always, that it produces a continual crop of timber. This is a point that is not always understood as the public watches the buying and cutting of timber. And it is one that is hard to maintain against the mounting pressure of "Give us more wood!"

Look at the National Forests in the Northern Region—more than twenty-six million acres. In that vast acreage, less than seventeen million acres are "commercial timber"; the remainder is nonforest land, such as national grasslands or wilderness where logging is prohibited. So here are nearly ten million acres—more than one third of the region—that do not and never will produce lumber.

Of course, seventeen million acres can produce a lot of lumber—for a time. And that "time" is so important—the need is so vital to stretch it, and stretch it, and stretch it still more—that today only 100,000 acres are harvested annually in the Northern Region. At this rate, complete logging will be spread over about 170 years.

Cut it faster? Perhaps. But look, too, at those thousand-dollar logs we saw on the truck back there. Douglas-fir, they were, three to six feet thick, from trees 200 feet tall or more. It will take from 200 to 250 years to replace them with trees of comparable size. If they were ponderosa pine, 400 to 500 years might be required.

Actually, under management in the Northern Region, the Forest Service estimates that the average tree being harvested there today could be grown in one third to one half the time it has taken to reach its present size. And, with all the region's timber areas under management and fully producing, foresters expect the annual harvest to climb to one percent, shortening the total cutover to less than 100 years. That figure seems re-

Clear-cut patches are ready for a new crop of trees.

markably short, in a forest of trees like these.

Southern forests, while smaller than those of the West, offer a better prospect for fast renewal; their trees grow faster and are easier reached for cultivation. But even here the pressure to cut the forests faster is steadily mounting.

Wood in almost any form brings a better price today than it has ever brought in our history. The marketers of wood want as much of it as they can get, to sell at these high prices. The users of wood seem never to have enough.

But if we cut the trees faster than they can grow, we will inevitably come to a time when we have no trees big enough to cut. So the managers of our timber hold the line—and more. They put important stress on producing more trees in every acre, and more wood in every tree.

Chapter 4

FOR BETTER TREES

High in the top of a lofty pine tree, a man is climbing, slowly, carefully.

The tree is taller, straighter, thicker than any of its neighbor trees. All the lower branches are gone. Its crown of living branches is thick and compact, a rich rounded cushion of green needles, high in the air.

The tree is one of the chosen ones—a Superior Tree.

What is going on here? Is the man a lumberjack, climbing the tree to top it, get it ready to be cut down? He is behaving very oddly for a lumberjack. In the first place, he is climbing with a ladder. Section by section, he pulls an aluminum ladder after him as he climbs, and boosts it up ahead of him. The only possible purpose of the ladder could be to protect the tree from the gashing cuts of a lumberjack's climbing spikes.

And the climber does not seem interested in cutting off the tree's top. The clippers he carries are smallish ones, with very long handles. The cutting job he is doing is very much more delicate than slashing off the top of the tree. Working now in the tree's crown, he is cutting here, there, and across from there. He pushes his clippers out to the very ends of the branches and nips off their tips, and the tips fall to the ground.

When the climber has finished with the tree, he will have from thirty to fifty branch tips waiting on the ground. He collects

A loblolly pine, chosen as a Superior Tree, is climbed by a forester to get scions. Using a ladder, he is careful not to damage the tree.

them, trims each one to about eight inches in length, and carefully packs them into plastic bags. He has tags that he marks with the species of tree and its number as a Superior Tree; he puts one of these tags inside each plastic bag and also ties one to the outside of each bag. No chance here to lose track of where these branch tips came from!

Why all this care with what were, until now, growing tips on a Superior Tree? These branch tips are "scions," a word meaning "descendants." In a sense, it is the key word for the tremendously exciting thing that is happening here: Descendants of Superior Trees are being collected, to produce a continuing line of descendants of Superior Trees. Year after year, they will be nurtured to produce thousands, millions, billions of offspring of their own, until, at some day in the future, forests may be made up of Superior Trees.

PRODUCING SUPERIOR TREES

The Superior Tree program has been under way in national forests for about ten years. A center for the program is the W. W. Ashe Nursery, on the De Soto National Forest near Brooklyn, Mississippi, where Superior Trees of the southern pines are being developed.

It took us several days of hard work to cover the "story" of the G. F. Erambert Seed Orchard near the Ashe Nursery. We went out on the forest to see for ourselves an original Superior Tree. We saw "orchards" and nurseries and seedbeds, each one filled with young, growing pine trees of uniform size. We saw rooms filled with files—stacks and stacks of meticulous reports and records. Every word in the reports, every seedling, every thriving young tree, is dedicated to the production of Superior Trees.

Foresters comb the woods to find the original Superior Trees. In a major forestry area, they select fifty, each one better than its neighbors—better for the production of lumber. In the South alone, 1,850 Superior Trees have been found and put to work.

Once found, such a tree is inspected several times by different experts before it is designated a Superior Tree. Then it is protected in every way that the Forest Service knows how to protect a tree—from cutting, from insects, and from disease. It is marked with a band of green paint, and a sign is placed at its base asking anyone who comes near it to help protect it.

How is a Superior Tree different from its neighbors? It must be perfectly straight, so that straight lumber could be cut from it without waste. It must be taller and larger than its neighbors, to produce as much lumber as possible. It must grow faster, to produce lumber at a faster rate. It must quickly drop its lower branches, so that they will not make big, wasteful knots in its wood.

Such a tree can hardly be transplanted into a nursery. But what is being done is, in effect, transplanting; the growing tips are being "transplanted." If straightness is their inheritance from the mother tree, straightness will be their own quality—and so on through the other qualities of quick, clean growth that they inherit.

So the scions come down and are shipped to a nursery. If they were clipped off in Mississippi, Alabama, or Florida, they are probably shipped to the Ashe Nursery.

In the nursery, meantime, thousands of seedlings are growing. These are pines, too, and the seeds from which they sprouted came from the same localities as the Superior Trees. They are kept sorted by kind of tree and by locality. They are the "rootstock," or the "understock." When they are about a foot-and-a-half high, they are ready to take their part in the production of Superior Trees.

Each scion coming into the nursery is grafted onto one of these seedlings—and not just anyone of them. Each scion is

The nurseryman clips the scion stem to a thin wedge, so that he can insert it into a slit he has made at the cut-off tip of the rootstock.

matched with a seedling that came from the same locality as the scion. A tree that grows from this union will be rich in fine qualities that it has inherited. Its roots will be adapted for growing in the soil of the locality from which both parts came. Its trunk and crown will have the vigorous qualities of the parent Superior Tree.

To graft a scion, it is cut to about four inches, and its stem is cut to a long, thin wedge. Then the top of the seedling rootstock is cut off and a slit is made in the remaining stalk. The scion stem is fitted into the slit, and the two are tightly bound together.

A plastic bag is pulled over each grafted scion, to keep it moist. Growth of a new tree now depends upon the knitting together of the rootstock stem and the scion stem. Will they knit? Now comes a thirty-day wait, when the nurserymen are in the anxious seat. They have done all they can, except to keep the graftlings moist. Row on row, the little trees stand in their containers, in a shed that has a plastic covering to hold moisture inside, and shade to keep the burning sun outside.

Cause for rejoicing is the first sign of new growth—the appearance of quarter-inch "pinfeathers" on the scion's tip. These are brand-new needles, and the baby tree is producing them on its own. They're a sure sign that moisture and nourishment are coming up from the new tree's roots and traveling into its stem —a sure sign that the knitting together of stems has taken place.

After the pinfeathers appear, the nurserymen poke holes in the plastic bags, so that the baby trees can gradually learn to live without the extra moisture from the bags. In about two weeks, the bags come off entirely. Meantime, the plastic covering of the shed has been coming off, two or three inches at a time. But shade over the shed still keeps out about half the normal sunshine.

Graftlings, covered with plastic bags, stand in a shed that protects them from the sun, while growth begins that will produce a Superior Tree.

This graftling has produced little knobs of "pinfeathers" at its tip.

In about two more weeks, the baby trees are ready to give up this sheltered life and move into the field. Into the soil they go, widely spaced and in orderly rows in "orchards" of several hundred acres.

Each one of these baby trees has been put together and coddled and coaxed to grow, with one idea in mind—to grow seeds. And not just ordinary seeds, but seeds that will produce Superior Trees.

TIME MUST PASS

It will take a while. Graftlings of the southern pines may grow four feet tall in one year, more than six feet tall in two. But they will be fifteen years old before they make cones and seeds—and several years older before they make their best cones.

It will take care. The orchards must be protected from insects, disease, and fire; the trees must be fed. And they must be protected from pollen of lesser trees. Only the pollen of a Superior Tree can pollinate a Superior Tree, if the seeds are to produce Superior Trees. So when the graftlings are planted, deep buffer zones are left around the orchards, to avoid lesser trees near the orchard. Graftlings from one locality are still kept separate from those of another.

When the seeds are harvested, the importance of this separation of localities becomes clear. The entire tree, you remember, is adapted to grow in the locality from which it came. So when its seeds are returned to the forests for planting, they will go back to the locality from which the tree came. Did the scion and rootstock that made these seeds come, originally, from southern Alabama? Then the seeds will go back to southern Alabama. Did they come from northern Florida? Then the seeds will be sent to northern Florida.

Back to the forests they will go, to replant national-forest acres that have been cut, or burned, or killed by disease—to plant new forests of trees that can produce far more lumber than today's ordinary forest trees.

The G. F. Erambert Seed Orchard covers 435 acres; it holds 36,000 grafted trees—Superior Trees. When we saw them, they were four years old, from grafting, and had already grown to heights of fifteen feet.

Every single one of these 36,000 trees was tagged with a card that numbered it, told its species, the locality it came from, the date it was grafted, the grafter's name, and the date it was planted. And back of each tree, in those voluminous files in the headquarters building, is a record of every detail about it, and about its parent Superior Tree and rootstock.

Pedigreed seeds will come from these 36,000 graftlings and from all the other thousands in seed orchards of other nurseries. Pedigreed, in vast quantities; the 36,000 graftlings could produce more than 500 million seeds in one year's crop. This would, of course, be a "good" year; many kinds of trees produce seeds in quantity only once in two or three or even five years. Although our figure is for a productive year, it gives some idea of the planting potential of the Superior Tree program.

The southern pines are a fine choice for the development of Superior Trees. They are relatively fast-growing; their native southland is warm and moist for growing trees. Systematic collection of scions and seed from them presents no great problems. So several other seed orchards have been planted in the South, and young grafted trees are growing there like weeds. On the Ouachita National Forest, shortleaf pines are growing in the 396-acre Ouachita Seed Orchard near Mt. Ida, Arkansas. They came, as scions, from 200 Superior Trees in the Ozarks National Forest of Arkansas, the Ouachita of Arkansas and Oklahoma, and the Mark Twain and the Clark of Missouri. When seeds develop, they will be returned to these localities, as seeds or seedlings.

In the 204-acre Stuart Orchard on Kisatchie National Forest, near Bentley, Louisiana, there are 20,000 young Superior Trees —Louisiana loblolly and longleaf, Texas loblolly and shortleaf.

In one way or another, all the national forests of the South are taking part in this program. But they do not, by any means, have a corner on it; it is under way in many places throughout the country—in Wisconsin and Michigan, in California and other western states.

In the great forests of Washington, Oregon, and California, Superior Trees of ponderosa pine and Douglas-fir tower from 200 to 350 feet tall. It is almost beyond possibility to climb these trees safely to secure scions. Even to reach the trees in the mountain forest is often difficult.

But our "helicopter age" has come to the rescue. Foresters are collecting scions here by helicopter. The copter hovers at the

A growing graftling is planted in its permanent place in the seed orchard.

tip of the tallest tree; a forester riding in the copter uses long-handled clippers to nip off each scion, hold onto it, and haul it in. He can collect fifteen scions in not more than four minutes; he can work fifteen trees in an hour, as against half a day for one tree if he were working from the ground. The scions are immediately refrigerated in the helicopter and are quickly flown to the nursery. Within four or five hours from the time they were cut, they have been grafted and are starting to grow into a "seed factory" for rugged mountain forests.

Hardwoods, too, are having their chance to produce Superior Trees; most recent development is a black cherry seed orchard on Allegheny National Forest in Pennsylvania.

And so it goes, throughout the country. Methods and numbers may differ, to fit the differing forests, but the purpose is the same everywhere: To improve the trees of every forest; to provide a never-ending supply of improved trees for every forest.

Today's foresters—the men who have developed this program

Two years after planting out, the graftling is a thriving young Superior Tree.

with faith and vision, patience and hard work—will not live long enough to see the new trees mature. On the forests, they told us again and again that the Superior Tree program is the most important aspect of forestry today. Yet not one of these men will ever see a mature forest of Superior Trees. Years must go by before the program shifts into high gear and the first seeds begin to come from the seed orchards. Once planted, a "fast-growing" southern pine must have from fifty to seventy years to grow large enough to make lumber. Clearly, this is a program whose benefits are a generation or more in the future. You, yourself, who have seen men walk the moon, will see forests of Superior Trees—and still may not see the trees mature. But your children will, and will use them to build their houses.

Foresters are not waiting for Superior Trees. They are planting more than 200 million new trees every year—trees that grow
from seeds and seedlings. Where do they get them?

Seeds come from the forests themselves and for many years
the methods of collecting them were somewhat hit-or-miss. They
must ripen, but if they are left too long on the trees, the cones
will open and the seeds will be lost. So, first of all, the foresters
must keep a close watch on the ripening cones. Southern foresters still rely on a long-used method of testing the cones. They
put a few cones in a five-gallon can that holds a gallon of motor
oil. If the cones float, they're mature and ready to pick.

So the Forest Service sends out the word—announcements in
newspapers, and on radio and television—and local people come
flocking to climb trees, knock off cones, and collect them. The
Forest Service pays them anywhere from fifty cents to six dollars
a bushel for the cones, depending on the kind of cone.

Seeds secured in this way are, of course, from trees of just
any quality. In some years there are many; in other years, few.
To get better seeds and to get them more evenly across the
years, the Forest Service has developed a new method.

Today, almost every forest has its own "seed production
area." This is a stand of mature, cone-producing trees, covering
anywhere from ten to forty acres. The stand was chosen because
it was rich in good trees—tall, straight, well-growing. The very
best of these were selected and marked—about twenty-five in
each acre. Then all other trees were removed, to give the best
ones room to grow, room for their crowns to spread out to make
cones and seeds. Moreover, this thinning helps to eliminate pollination from inferior trees. So seed production in these areas
is greatly increased, and the seeds come from good trees.

This is a long step in the same direction as Superior Trees, and it was immediately productive. The seed production areas are today bearing the burden of supplying hundreds of thousands of pounds of seeds for reforestation, all over the country. They will continue to do so until the Superior Tree seed orchards are well along in the production of seeds.

The method is being extended to hardwoods. In the Hoosier National Forest in southern Indiana, a seed production area was recently established to grow seeds for black walnut.

What happens after the seed-bearing pine cones are collected? They go into nurseries all over the country—the Ashe Nursery, the Coeur d'Alene Nursery in Idaho, the big Eveleth and Chittenden nurseries of Minnesota and Michigan, and many others. In general, they go to the nursery nearest the area where they were collected. Every lot is kept separate from the lots coming from other forestry areas, because here, again, seeds and seedlings are returned to the area where the seeds grew.

Coming into the nursery, the cones are dried in heated kilns until they open; as many as 2,000 bushels of cones can be dried at a time. Then the seeds are shaken from them, cleaned, and put into cold storage. Sometimes they are used within a few months; but some kinds of seeds will keep for several years in cold storage, and so a "bank" can be built up for use in years when few cones form.

Before the seeds are planted, they are treated at the nursery with a repellent that keeps birds and rodents from eating them. Then some of them are returned, on demand, to the forest from which they came. They will be planted in the open forest from planes and helicopters, or inserted in the earth by machines.

By far the greatest part of the nurseries' work is with the seeds they keep. These seeds they plant in great beds; each bed has only one species of tree, from one specified forest area. In one year or two or three, the little seedling trees are ready to be transplanted into the forest. And the foresters are ready for

Foresters working in a helicopter take scions from a Douglas-fir in an Oregon national forest.

them, their work carefully scheduled years in advance.

Millions on millions of the little seedlings are produced each year. In the Eastern Region alone, about fifteen million young trees are planted annually in the national forests. The Chittenden Nursery near Wellston, Michigan, ships three million red pine seedlings a year to the forests of this region, especially to those of lower Michigan. The Eveleth Nursery, near Cass Lake, Minnesota, supplies seedlings for the great pine and spruce forests of Minnesota.

These activities are repeated the country over in national forest nurseries. Coeur d'Alene can ship eighteen million seed-

Workers pollinate white pine conelets with pollen from rust-resistant trees. (A mature cone from last year hangs at the left.)

lings a year; two nurseries in California, Humboldt and Placerville, ship sixteen million ponderosa, Jeffrey, and sugar pine, red and white fir, and Douglas-fir. Nurseries at Bend, Oregon, and Wind River, Washington, each supply fifteen million Douglas-fir and ponderosa pine seedlings for planting in these Pacific Northwest states. The Mt. Sopris Nursery near Basalt, Colorado, sends thirty million seedlings to the forests of the Rocky Mountain Region. And in the South, thirty million seedlings go to southern forests anywhere from Texas to Virginia.

Sometimes a nursery is especially concerned with a particular problem in its own locality. The Bessey Nursery on the Nebraska National Forest, for example, supplies all the trees for the plantations of the Bessey Division of this forest—the largest man-made forest in the world. Every tree in the Bessey Division has been planted by man, originally to provide fence posts and firewood for pioneer settlers. Today the Bessey Nursery supplies seedlings to Nebraska farmers and ranchers for planting shelterbelts and windbreaks, and to the state for conservation programs.

While all this is going on, millions on millions of seeds and seedlings are being planted on state forests by state forestry agencies, and on privately owned forest land. They come largely from state and private nurseries, although special arrangements are often made for a national forest nursery to grow seedlings for a state; and sometimes a state nursery grows seedlings for a national forest.

RESEARCH LEADS TO BETTER TREES

Back of the nurseries and seed orchards—back of the whole great job of tree improvement and replanting, and all the other improvement and management of the forests—is a fabulous program of research. An army of men and women, scientists all, are working year after year, testing, investigating, experimenting. This is a nationwide detective force, bent on sleuthing out the best methods and materials with which to improve the forests.

Do eastern foresters want to know the effect on their trees of soil quality—or of insects and disease, or storms, or drought? They can turn to the research projects of the Northeastern Forest Experiment Station, headquartered in Upper Darby, Pennsylvania. Do southern foresters need to know the percentage of seeds in any year that will germinate and produce seedlings? They ask the Eastern Tree Seed Laboratory in Macon, Georgia. Do westerners need the newest information on successful planting of larch and Engelmann spruce? They can get it from the Forestry Sciences Laboratory at Missoula, Montana, which keeps close check on these trees in several experimental forests.

Research throughout the nation is in the front line of the tremendous battle against disease and damaging insects. When an epidemic of tussock moths swept through hundreds of thousands of acres of Douglas-firs and true firs in the Pacific states, research teams in the Malheur and Ochoco national forests of Oregon worked around the clock to discover an amount of DDT that could be used for spraying and still not damage the watersheds and the wildlife of the forests. Later, a virus spray that is deadly to the larvae of the tussock moth, but affects only that one insect, was developed in Oregon laboratories. In the Rockies it is hoped that a poison has been developed that will be deadly to spruce budworm, yet will not affect wildlife.

Blister rust, surviving every poison that the laboratories have been able to produce, has almost wiped out America's white pines. But research may still have a hopeful answer. Many research centers are concerned with genetic improvement—that is, with producing better trees by controlling their inheritance, as in the Superior Tree program. And in many of these genetic projects, rust-resistant strains of white pines are being developed.

In Washington and Oregon more than 400 rust-resistant white

Beds of ponderosa pine seedlings are kept weeded and watered at Coeur d'Alene Nursery in Idaho.

pines have been found growing in the forests. Foresters are working with them to control pollination and, therefore, the inherited characteristics that are passed along to their seeds. Climbers go into the trees, find branchlets with several cones, and cover them with plastic bags. When it is time for the cones to be pollinated, the workers use hypodermic needles to inject pollen from other rust-resistant trees. So the seeds' inheritance is fully that of rust resistance. In this way, the experimenters hope to secure seeds that will produce new trees with dependable, built-in resistance to the killing rust.

From the Forestry Sciences Laboratory at Moscow, Idaho, comes the latest word on a twenty-five-year-old project to develop a rust-resistant western white pine. The first seedlings from orchard-grown, rust-resistant seeds have just been put into the ground in St. Joe National Forest. Their success against rust could insure the life of the western white pine.

Other genetic projects, countrywide, are also concerned with producing rust-resistant white pines, including the sugar pine, and with improving kinds of trees to make them more hardy and more disease-resistant. A leader in this research is the Institute of Forest Genetics at Placerville, California, where a big collection of pine hybrids—crosses—of various kinds has been developed. Better-growing stock for forests of the future will come from these hybrids.

In the South, the slash pine is fast growing and has good roots, but is easily damaged by cold weather. The shortleaf pine, also a southern native, is not hurt by ice and cold. So experiments in genetics in the South include producing a hybrid or "cross" of these two trees that will have the good qualities of both.

The research job is not only to produce better trees, but to produce better forests. In all the factors of forest management, research is helping to find the answers to problems that are both urgent and important. At Missoula, Montana, the Northern Forest Fire Laboratory studies everything from lightning and fuels to smoke jumpers. There are scores of laboratories, experimental watersheds, and experimental forests that provide information to help solve all kinds of forestry problems.

More than a dozen projects are measuring the effect of air pollution on forests. Many of the 336 Natural Areas recently set aside for research by Federal agencies are projects manned and managed by the Forest Service. These include various experimental forests, ranges, and other areas where trees, range forage, and wildlife are under observation.

Nor does research stop with the National Forest Service. Universities and colleges all over the country are working more or less in partnership with the Forest Service to produce information promptly. The Forestry Sciences Laboratory in Missoula cooperates closely with scientists at the University of Montana. In Madison, Wisconsin, the Forest Products Laboratory works with the University of Wisconsin. In California, this kind of cooperation has recently made history in the battle against bark beetles, several different kinds of which have destroyed count-less thousands of acres of ponderosa pines, spruce, firs, Douglas-firs, and other forest trees.

The beetles can, most of the time, withstand spraying; they are under the bark and in the wood of the tree, where sprays do not reach. But when they mate, they come to the surface and are then vulnerable to spraying. The California laboratories have put together a chemical that attracts the male beetles, bringing them to the surface. By using this chemical as bait, foresters can trap the beetles in great numbers, and may be able, eventually, to get rid of them.

Results are shared with state forests, with private forest owners, with industries—with all those working in such fields as watersheds, wildlife, range improvement, fire protection, and recreation. It is a published goal of the Forest Service "to inten-sify research programs that will advance the wise use of all forest and related resources throughout America." Typical of this policy is the Alexandria Forestry Center at Alexandria, Louisiana, where management and research in national, state, and private forestry are located together in one big center.

Eight regional Forest and Range Experiment Stations head up the whole research job for the National Forests. They are located at Ogden, Utah; Berkeley, California; Fort Collins, Colorado; Portland, Oregon; St. Paul, Minnesota; Upper Darby, Pennsyl-vania; Asheville, North Carolina; and New Orleans, Louisiana. They organize and direct the work of the hundreds of labora-tories and field locations, all seeking the knowledge that can make "Forests Forever" a reality.

Chapter 5

FIRE!

Flames leaped upward into the tops of trees in a frightening explosion. Heat from them, smoke from them made the ground a nightmare, where two men worked desperately.

The two, Jim and Jake, were "smokejumpers" from the Forest Service firefighters. They had been jumped at daylight by parachute, to the vicinity of this small fire on a mountainside. Each with a pulaski—a hoe on the back of an axe—and with shovels and other tools parachuted from the plane, they struggled to put out as much fire as they could and to clear a space ahead of it—a fire line. Across this, they hoped, the fire would not go.

A helicopter had crossed and recrossed, spraying a mixture of water and chemicals, thickened with clay—a "slurry"—to reduce the fire. It had helped, but it had missed an especially hot spot. The wind was high and getting higher, and as flames leaped upward to the tops of the trees, the two men knew they could not control it with a fire line. Burning brands were already traveling upward and streaking out ahead, starting new fires wherever they fell.

Jim and Jake had been jumped here as soon as it was light enough for them to see, in response to a fire-patrol plane's report of a small fire. During the night a "dry" electric storm had swept through the mountains—a storm with crashing lightning and thunder, but no rain; there had been no rain for weeks. On

A smokejumper drops to a fire, pulling on the lines of his parachute to guide it to the spot where he wants to land.

Helicopters cross and recross the forest ahead of a fire, dropping slurry from tanks attached underneath them.

the heels of the storm, the patrol plane was up and checking, because a storm like this can start dozens of fires in a forest—a forest so dry that a spark will set it off.

The patrol plane did not have to wait for daylight. It was equipped with an infrared sensor that even in darkness could detect the tiniest of fires. It had reported numerous small fires, and a team of smokejumpers had quickly gone to each one.

Jim stood now for a few seconds, watching the flames leap toward them. Smoke hung close, clouding his view of everything except what was near. The crackling of the flames was very loud and almost shrill, and with it he could hear an accompanying roar and an occasional sharp, crashing report as a tree literally exploded. Over and above all these, he could hear, or thought he could hear, a deeper, heavier roar that seemed to come from all outdoors, from the ground itself. It sounded, he thought, like the whole doggone mountain was afire. Could be, too, because all he had to go on was sound, since they were shut in by smoke.

But they were not cut off. Jim had already used his two-way radio to ask for reinforcements. Now he knew that reinforcements would be no help. And even as he reached to his belt for the radio to say so, it buzzed, and the fire boss spoke rapidly in his ear.

"Jim, you and Jake get out of there, fast. There's a big fire coming around the mountain straight at you, and she's off and running. You got the knoll you jumped on spotted?"

"Yeah."

"Okay, a copter is making for it. You guys get there but quick, you hear?"

"Roger."

Stopping only to grab up tools, Jim and Jake scrambled for the knoll. Their parachutes were there, spread out where they had fallen. The two men were dead tired, but they worked like demons to roll up the chutes. They had only a few seconds before the copter would sit down, and they were determined to get the chutes aboard. A smokejumper abandons his chute to a fire even more reluctantly than a sailboater lets his boat sink.

In a moment or two the helicopter was sitting down, and Jim and Jake threw in the chutes and their tools and climbed aboard. Then they were up again, and the two men's eyes widened as they looked at the mountainside below them. In truth, the fire was "off and running." Almost the whole mountain was covered with rolling billows of smoke, shot through with torches of flame that appeared here, there, and there again as fire exploded upward in the trees and spread through the crowns. As they watched, a flaming sea engulfed the little knoll where the helicopter had picked them up.

Their pilot filled them in. More than twenty fires had been

started by the lightning of the night before. Some of them had merged, and the rising wind had brought fire around the mountain with unbelievable speed.

Smokejumpers, four, six, eight, and more men to a team, had jumped along the flanks of the fire, to try to keep it from creeping down or climbing higher along the mountainside. But putting it out now, against the wind, would require an all-out massing of forces at a strategic point. Miles ahead, the mountainside swept up to a high ridge where a logging road ran, climbing from towns at the foot of the mountain. Here the firefighters were already making their stand.

There were ridges between this spot and the fire, where trees and brush were sparser and the fire would tend to slow a little. Planes traveled above them and sprayed slurry across the fire's path. The clay in this soupy mix made it cling wetly to trees and brush, a fire-resistant coating. It would slow the flames, and so the battle on the high ridge ahead might be won.

The helicopter took Jim and Jake to an emergency fire camp at the foot of the ridge, which had been speedily set up near the road as the firefighters' headquarters. They found the camp boiling with activity. Trucks were rolling in from the towns below, loaded with men and tools, with chemicals and food. Many were pulling out again on the road to the ridge, swarming with men and heavy with equipment. Some had power tools aboard—saws and trenchers, which would do the work of several men in cutting and digging a wide fire line. Bulldozers pulled in, and followed up the road to the ridge.

Helicopters were landing, picking up a full tank of slurry to replace an empty one, and taking off again. Ground tanks, already on trucks for transportation to the ridge, were being filled with slurry.

Machines were a wonderful, modern advantage in this great battle. But in the final test, it would be men who put out the

Fire can leap from the top of one tree to another and it can creep along the ground in dry litter, to climb the trees.

fire—men and more men. It took men to run the machines, to prepare and load slurry. Most of the tools aboard the trucks were hand tools—pulaskis and axes and shovels; tools that men would use to beat and smother fire, by hand.

So the call had gone out—and was being answered—for every man who could help.

A "kitchen" had been quickly set up at the camp; hard-working men must have food to keep them going. Here Jake and Jim had a quick meal and a cup of coffee, along with many others. Then, assigned to a ground crew, they were on a truck and traveling up to the ridge.

On the ridge, a wide fire line was taking shape. Trees and brush were being cleared from both sides of the road, and helicopters worked overhead to spread slurry in an ever-widening path. Truck tankers filled with water and chemicals stood beside the road, for use when the fire came closer.

Crews had been scattered ahead, to put out small spot fires started by burning brands. One small fire was doing its best to get started just beyond the road; Jim and Jake and their crew pounced on it and put it out by swiftly shoveling dirt onto it. Then they joined in the task of widening the fire line.

The first of the flames came up the ridge, reached the slurry, and slowed. But they found, here and there, brush that would burn, and came on. Men met them with ground tanks and pack tanks, and with shoveled dirt, and put them out.

But now, with frightening suddenness, the main burn was upon them. Flames leaped and roared a few feet from the fire line. Trees burned all the way back through the forest, as far as the men could see. The overhead attack had slowed down the fire, but the flames came on persistently. The firefighters could easily "lose" the fire here—it could jump the line and sweep on and on through the forest.

Planes and helicopters continued to drop slurry from over-

Billowing clouds of smoke show the extent of a fire on a mountainside.

head. The men on the ground emptied tanks into the fire and shoveled endlessly, to douse the flames that burned there. Here a crew was losing a long tongue of flame that ran, somehow, deep into the fire line. Quickly a tanker and more shovelers came to help. All along the line, men moved back and forth, spreading out where the fire was light, concentrating where the flames were thickest.

At last they were gaining on the flames near the fire line. The ground was blackened and ashy and smoldering, and some of the trees smoldered, but the fire was being controlled. The men worked farther and farther into the forest, putting out fire as they went. Some of them would go on working through the night. Others would snatch a few hours' rest at the camp and return, by dawn, to relieve those still at the fire.

Bulldozers knock down vegetation and spread raw earth to build a fire line.

Many would work again through the blackened, smoking forest, to "mop up." This was an operation that might continue, on all sides, for several days or a week. It would be finished only when fire no longer burned anywhere in the forest.

THE GREATEST FIREFIGHTERS

All this was a far cry from firefighting in the early days of the Forest Service. There were many years of trying to control and put out fires when firefighters hiked into the forest or rode by mule train, their food and equipment back-packed or packed onto the mules. There were no trucks or planes or helicopters or tanks filled with chemicals; no two-way radios or infrared sensors or smokejumpers or crews trained to work together.

In 1910, the worst fire year on record, 1,582 fires in Montana and Idaho alone burned 3,200,000 acres of national forests.

In 1967, the worst year since 1910, 1,851 fires burned 83,000 acres of national forests in the Northern Region. More fires in 1967—but only a small fraction of the acreage burned. In the meantime, the Forest Service has been developing what has been called "the greatest firefighting organization in the world." It has three elements: manpower, equipment, and communication.

The intervening years had brought their fires, but the 1967 season was so bad, especially in the northwestern states, that western foresters call it "The Fire Year." There was no general rainfall from the latter part of July through August and September. The forests dried out, and even the air was dry; temperatures were high, day and night. For the first time in history, forests were closed to visitors and loggers alike, from the Continental Divide in Montana westward across Idaho, Oregon, and Washington to the Pacific. For fifty-nine consecutive days, the Forest Service reported "very high" and "extreme" fire danger.

August brought dry lightning storms—and lightning starts

Firefighters use hand tools to put out fire on the ground.

more than 80 percent of the forest fires in the Northern Region. Everywhere lightning struck, it started a fire. The first of these storms set 167 fires, and on each of two other days, set more than 100; many days saw fifty new fires. Thousands of men battled them day and night, and were successful in putting out many. But, from August 11 to September 10, fifty-three major fires burned on the forests of the Northern Region, all of them for several days, some of them for much of that period.

These were the dates for the biggest one of all—the Sundance fire. The Sundance was so violent and so disastrous that foresters measure other fires against it. Started by lightning southeast of the Kaniksu National Forest in northern Idaho, it swept across 56,000 acres of privately owned and national forest before it was finally stopped deep on the Kaniksu. It had everything it needed. Pushed by high winds, the flames built up the deadly "fire whirls" that are, in fact, fire tornadoes—winds that whirl at 300 miles an hour and lift trees bodily from the ground. The fire took everything before it. In a single day and night it covered almost eighty square miles, licking up a square mile of timber in as little as three minutes.

Several thousand men worked along its perimeter and manned the aircraft that kept up a continual drop of water and chemical retardants. But it took them days on end to bring the Sundance under control, and it was almost another month, with rain helping, before they could complete the mopping up.

MANPOWER

So here is the manpower—the men who continue to fight in the face of terrible odds, until they win. Some 13,000 of them were mobilized that summer from all over the West; more than 7,000 were on the fire lines at one time.

They came from nearby homes and loggers' camps, from other national forests near and far, from state forests, from the

Men come by truck and car to a point near the fire, and move on the run to a spot that is burning.

Army and the Air Force and the National Guard, from the National Park Service, from the Job Corps, from other national agencies. Eskimos came from the far north, and Indians came from their reservations—Navajos, Sioux, Cheyennes, Apaches, and many others. Forests not themselves involved with fire became recruiting stations. By plane, bus, car, and truck, men poured into the firefighting headquarters.

Assignment desks were set up in the hotels of major cities, to get the men on their way to fires. Camps were set up near the fires to feed them and provide a place to rest. These men would work long hours on the fire lines—ten to twelve hours at a stretch, sometimes as many as eighteen hours.

Most of them had fought fire before. Often they were recruited in organized crews; and many of the crews were groups of foresters and others who had been given special training by the Forest Service in fighting fire on the ground. In a Forest Service report they were commended for their "ability to lead, to attack independently, to respond to instructions, and to provide that additional effort frequently needed. They responded quickly and willingly to the demands made upon them this season."

THE SMOKEJUMPERS

Especially trained, too, are the smokejumpers, who, like Jim and Jake, parachute from plane to fire. They jump in teams of never less than two, the number determined by the job ahead; the average team is four or five, but many are ten to twenty-five. Once, more than sixty were jumped to one assignment. They go into roadless areas where there is no other access. They go quickly to a small fire, to put it out or at least to keep it from growing to a large fire while the slower ground crews are getting there. They go to the edges of a big fire, to

Smokejumpers, suited up and ready to go.

hold it back while ground crews are arriving. In the whole United States, during the fire season of 1967, these men made 7,358 jumps.

Smokejumpers are trained not only in firefighting but in jumping—taught to land unhurt on rocky hillsides and in thick timber, taught to steer their parachutes to land accurately and easily. They learn survival techniques. They learn to "suit up," board their planes, fully equipped, in not more than twenty minutes; a departure is often accomplished in much less time.

The number of smokejumpers has climbed to nearly 500; about 200 are trained at the Forest Service Aerial Fire Depot near Missoula, Montana, where the smokejumping operation has been underway for more than thirty years. Others are trained at other bases in all of the western regions—big ones such as those at Redmond Air Center and Cave Junction, Oregon, and the North Cascades base near Winthrop, Washington.

New men get four weeks' training, making at least seven practice jumps. Many have returned from a previous year, and they take a week's refresher course. From late spring to early fall, the men live on base and are always on call. Some go to smaller bases in the region, and some are loaned from time to time to other regions that are fighting big fires. And, as in 1967, the other regions send help to Missoula when it is needed. Wherever the smokejumpers are, their lives are dominated by the looming obligation to fight fire the next hour, the next day, the next week.

Many of these men are college students and teachers interested in forestry, but they come from all walks of life and from all parts of the country. To be accepted for training, each one must have a season's previous experience in fire control and must pass a rigorous test for physical fitness. In addition, the Forest Service learns as much as they can about each man. Is he reliable? Resourceful? Will he work under stress? Can he face danger? These are qualities that can mean life and death, not only to the jumper himself but to others working with him.

EQUIPMENT

To jump a fire, a smokejumper wears a padded, fireproof white nylon suit and a helmet with a face shield. There is a parachute packed on his back and a smaller one on his chest, in case the big one fails. In a huge pocket on one leg of his suit he carries a ladder of nylon webbing ("bird nest" to him) for a let-down rope, in case he lands in the top of a tall tree. The rope is braided a special way, so that it unreels as he needs it and doesn't tangle. (The jumpers call it "braiding," but any woman knows that it is simply "crocheted" into a single-stitch chain—the world's best device for preventing snarling.) Also in leg pockets are signaling devices, a bag for the parachute, and extra batteries for the radio on the jumper's belt. Fully dressed, the smokejumper's official name is "Oscar."

Several packages are dropped to the jumpers by parachute, after a jump is completed. They contain tools, drinking water, food, sleeping bags—whatever the jumpers will need for several days of firefighting. There is even an aluminum-foil tent that can be quickly set up to shelter them against fire. When a fire has been put out by smokejumpers, they take their tools and equipment to a trail and leave them to be picked up. But they carry their personal gear to the nearest road, where they are picked up by a truck.

After a parachute has been used, the smokejumper returns it to the base for inspection and repair; any break in it of more than three threads is mended. It is dried and brushed free of debris such as pine needles and sand—and of passengers such as snakes and mice, unlikely but occasionally present.

Here, then, is equipment—devices and materials that enable men to get to a fire quickly, and to fight it successfully and

A seaplane drops water from a tank between its pontoons, on a fire on Superior National Forest, in Minnesota.

safely. Equipment ranges from the new, highly technical infrared sensor to the homely, time-tried pulaski and shovel; it includes such extensive facilities as dormitories and smoke-jumper training areas.

Planes and helicopters, as we have seen, carry not only men and tools, but fire-retardant liquids. Sometimes, if a lake is nearby, the liquid may be only water, dumped from a "sling bucket" that dangles below a helicopter; after the bucketload is dumped, the helicopter goes back to a nearby lake for a refill. Result: A giant bucket brigade, especially if several helicopters are at work at the same time.

Because lakes are everywhere in Superior National Forest, seaplanes are used there for firefighting; they can land on a lake with firefighters and equipment, near almost any fire. Here, they are the bucket brigade. They have tanks fitted between their pontoons, and when they taxi across a lake, they scoop up water as they go. They fly over the fire, dump the water on it, and return to the lake for more.

There are several other kinds of tanks in use—big 500-gallon ones on trucks, middle-size ones on wheels, smaller ones for back-packing. For the slurry that fills the tanks, the chemical is often a fertilizer—for example, a phosphate. Fertilizers not only have proved to be good fire retardants, but they serve the double purpose of improving the forest soil. Chemicals go to the fire camps by truck and by helicopter; planes pick up the slurry, prepared and waiting, at air fields where it is stored in huge tanks. There are more than thirty "chemical retardant bases" at strategic points, where planes can be loaded.

There are pumps and hoses that can bring water from a nearby lake or stream. There are lights working on high-power batteries, to bring greater safety and efficiency to firefighting at night. There are insulated sleeping bags made of paper, so inexpensive that a man can throw one away after using it. There are portable kitchens, and special meals to be prepared in them; one is a frozen, precooked meal in a plastic bag. Fifty or more of these can be packed in a "steamer"—a big metal barrel—and dropped to a crew from the air. They are heated for eating by putting water into the bottom of the barrel and setting it over any open fire.

The infrared sensor, or scanner, is perhaps the most glamorous and certainly one of the most valuable aids that the firefighters have. From a plane 15,000 feet overhead, it can spot a fire only twelve inches in diameter, exactly pinpointing the location. The scanner "sees" in the dark as well as in daylight. Flown over a smoke-blanketed forest, it can "see" through heavy smoke to find the exact outlines of a fire and to locate with absolute accuracy the hottest parts. It can find dangerous "hot spots" in a burned-over forests where the fire seems to be out. Foresters believe they have only begun to make use of this fine new tool.

The instrument panel of the infrared sensor, in a patrol plane. At the right, the operator is checking his photographs against a map of the forest.

In the meantime, patrol planes and tall fire lookout towers at high points are also in use on almost every forest.

COMMUNICATION

Best use of the sensor, of course, requires quick reporting of its findings; and here is the use of our third major element—communication. Reports from the sensor in a patrol plane over a fire are radioed within seconds to the fire chief who is directing the firefighting, perhaps in a helicopter also over the fire. By radio, he passes along this information, with instructions, to the crews on the ground and to the planes and helicopters that are spreading slurry. So a fire can often be kept from intensifying because the hottest spots receive attention first, and can often be kept from spreading because the workers are informed of the spread and can stop it almost before it happens.

On-the-spot communication, important as it is, is only part of the communication story. From the time a fire is reported, uncounted messages fly out and back, by radio, by telephone, by tickertape; they report, give instructions, ask for help. An army of people, women as well as men, many of them volunteers, work day and night to keep these messages cleared.

PREVENTING FIRE

To firefighters and everyone else connected with forest fires, preventing fire is very much better than putting it out. The best known symbol of forest-fire prevention is "Smokey the Bear," whose slogans, "Keep America Green" and "Prevent Forest Fires," are known to everyone who has visited a forest in the past few years. Smokey and his shovel have been pictured far and wide in connection with such warnings as "Break your matches," "Drown your campfires," "Be careful with *every* fire." He has done a world of good; foresters credit him with a large share of the substantial decrease in man-made fires. On page 163 you can read the story of how Smokey, when he was just a cub, became a firefighter.

In the West, lightning starts far more fires than man. Smokey can't help much in prevention of lightning fires, but there are other precautions that the Forest Service uses. One of these is getting rid of slash—that huge accumulation of branches that are trimmed off the tree trunks when an area is logged. Even before it dries, slash is a fire hazard, and foresters try to clear it out before the fire season starts.

With new machinery and processes, more slash every year is being used for wood products—for chipping, crushing, or pulverizing, to make various kinds of pressed wood; chips are

Only prevention can help this forest resident. When the forest burns, his nesting tree is destroyed.

often used for mulch and landscaping. But to get rid of most of it, foresters still must depend upon burning—very carefully controlled and guarded burning, at a time when the surrounding forest will not be endangered.

Aimed at lightning itself, experiments are being conducted in the Northern Region to "seed" or "ice-out" a cloud, so that it will no longer produce an electric charge. Silver iodide goes into the cloud from an airplane and causes the water in it to freeze to ice; the cloud then feathers out and blows away. If this operation can be carried through on a large scale, it is possible that storms can be stopped before they get started.

"Foehn winds" are another element of weather that greatly increases the danger of fire. They are the "Chinook winds" of Montana, the "devil winds" of southern California—great air masses from high altitudes that sweep down, hot and dry. When a foehn wind comes, foresters know that a fire is going to be hard to control.

RESEARCH FIGHTS FIRE

Back of all the operations for preventing, detecting, and putting out fire, as well as making it serve a useful purpose, is information that comes from national forest laboratories—some of the finest scientific laboratories in the world. One of these is the Northern Forest Fire Laboratory near Missoula; there are various others in other regions. They cooperate closely with science departments of universities and with other agencies nation-wide, to investigate firefighting and fire prevention.

To a fire-laboratory researcher, the trees and other plants on a forest are, first of all, "fuels"—the things that will burn if fire attacks the forest. The laboratory investigates the "fuel science" of a forest, examining the different kinds of trees and brush and grass. How quickly does each kind of plant catch fire? How fast does it burn? What effect does its age have? The answers can tell a fire chief what to expect by way of speed and intensity as a fire burns.

Fuel science is only one branch of the laboratories' investigations. What turns little fires into big ones? What makes some fires "blow up"? What is the best retardant to use, under a given set of conditions? How does weather affect fires? How can men and equipment be used more effectively, and more safely, to fight fires? The laboratories are building a substantial base of answers to such questions.

They are improving the use of that little genie of almost-magic, the infrared sensor. They developed cloud seeding, and are working on better materials and methods. They are investigating new possibilities for using slash, and better ways to burn it. They are exploring the possibility of feeding fire-retardant fertilizers to trees and other forest plants to make them fire resistant—and they remind us that tobacco growers control the rate of burning by the fertilizers they use.

Some of their knowledge assists the comeback that a forest makes after a fire; they know what fire does to the acidity and quality of soil, and what plants will prosper in a given burned area. Using a solid base of laboratory research, foresters re-seeded after the Sundance fire while the ashes were still hot. They planted rye grass and other recommended grasses, shrubs, and trees. In the words of one of them, "The comeback is unbelievable—the forest is making a fantastically fast recovery." He compares it with another large area burned eight years ago, and reports that Sundance already has more vegetation.

In general, foresters know that in fifteen years a new forest is on its way, the undergrowth well established, young conifers coming. It may well be that the fire laboratories are supplying knowledge that can greatly reduce that figure. It may be that burned-over areas of the future can duplicate the rapid comeback of the Sundance.

Chapter 6

A HOME FOR WILDLIFE

Squeak! Squeak! Squeak!

The tiny, yet piercing, sound seemed to come from near at hand—then at some distance. We sat quietly on a large rock at the edge of a rockslide near timberline on the Uncompahgre National Forest in Colorado. And waited. Soon the sound came again, quite close this time. We looked intently at the place where the squeaking seemed to originate, and in a minute or so we spied the squeaker—a small, brownish-gray animal that looked somewhat like an undersize guinea pig. Its color had blended so perfectly with the rocks around it that we had failed to see it at first.

As we watched, the squeaking sound came again, at a distance, and we discovered that this little animal was doing a ventriloquist act—it was making all the sounds, both at a distance and close at hand! Suddenly we realized that here was something we had heard about all our lives but had never seen—the pika, or cony as it is sometimes called, or rock rabbit.

We had also heard it called the "little haymaker," and soon found out why. After a few minutes, it apparently decided we were just a part of our rock, and came slowly off its rock, looking around cautiously. Finally it began scurrying around, cutting off tall blades of grass and stems of flowers and other

Wild turkey—this all-American bird inhabits every national-forest region in the nation except Alaska, but is not found in every forest. By far the greater numbers are in the South and Southwest.

101

plants until it had collected all it could carry in its mouth. Then it ran to a small pile of dried grass and weeds between some rocks and added its mouthful to the pile, carefully spreading it in a thin layer. The little haymaker was harvesting its winter food and piling it in "shocks" to dry, much as a farmer harvests his hay.

The pika does not hibernate during the winter, nor can it make tunnels through the snow. So it must dry its "crop" of grass and weeds and flowers and then store it underground.

A miniature relative of the hares and rabbits, the pika doesn't look much like them because it has short, rounded ears and hardly any tail; its hind legs are the same length as its forelegs.

As we started to leave, a slight noise drew our attention to a high crag above our heads. There stood one of the most magnificent animals in the high-altitude forests—a bighorn ram. Spellbound, we gazed up at him and he looked down at us, seeming to know that he was safe on his rocky crag. Then he bounded away, leaping from rock to rock with no effort at all. As we watched, he was joined by several ewes, and they all disappeared among the rocks.

The sight was a real thrill to us, for we had not seen any bighorns, or mountain sheep, since we were youngsters in southwestern Colorado. Then a band of bighorns, their natural timidity overcome by hunger, came down every winter from the high mountains on this same forest to the little town of Ouray. They foraged for bits of hay around the freight yards, where it had been dropped from shipments, and even climbed into the boxcars looking for it. People fed them, too, and the animals forgot their shyness. One became so bold that it ate an apple pie a woman had set in an open window to cool.

These handsome sheep have hair like that of a deer, instead of wool like a domestic sheep. The ram's horns, which rise up and back from the head and then curl forward in almost a com-

plete circle, are a prize for any sportsman. The horns do not drop
off the way a buck's antlers do, but continue to grow year after
year. The ewe also has horns, which are short and sharp-pointed,
a good defense against predators that try to steal her lamb.

Bighorns, found only in the West, may weigh anywhere from
125 to 250 pounds; an extra large ram can weigh 300 pounds.
Their color varies according to the locality where they live. The
Rocky Mountain bighorns are light to dark brown, with a white
rump; desert bighorns are a light sandy color, much like their
surroundings. Bighorns in Alaska, Dall sheep, are white.

Bighorns' hoofs are divided into two parts, like those of a
cow. They have sharp edges around cushiony pads that do not
slip when the sheep leaps from rock to rock, or travels up and
down the sides of steep cliffs.

In the summer, bighorns frequent the summits of high mountains, where they have few enemies and where grass, their favorite food, is plentiful. But in the winter, the snow is so deep that
they cannot scrape it away with their horns and hoofs, and they
usually come down to lower levels. Here, alas, the story is different. Deer and elk often feed at the lower levels, too, and
sometimes domestic sheep are pastured here. So the bighorns
have to eat whatever they can find. They dig up what food they
can from under the snow, and they browse on low-growing
shrubs. Some of them die from hunger or from parasites or
disease that they get from domestic sheep. Some are killed by
predators or hunters.

At the beginning of the last century, there were probably
between one and two million bighorns in this country. Today
the number is in the thousands. Bighorns are rigidly protected
in most of the states where they live. However, where the number in any particular locality becomes too large for the feed
available, carefully managed special hunts are conducted.

Enough winter range to sustain the bighorns seems to be the

most important factor now in their preservation. Excluding domestic sheep and cattle and sharp reduction of deer and elk from the winter range, as well as restoration of overgrazed vegetation, are ways of increasing range for the bighorns.

FROM INSECTS TO MOOSE

Many of the species of wildlife in the United States can be found in the national forests, from myriads of tiny insects to huge mammals such as the moose and the Alaska brown bear. Some of the insects are very destructive—aphids and pine beetles and the larvae of tussock moths and others; some insects are helpful, because they prey on the destructive ones.

Take that gay little ladybird beetle (also called ladybug), with her red wing-covers and black dots—remember how we used to chant, when we saw one: "Ladybird, ladybird, fly away home. Your house is on fire, your children will burn"? Well, that little beetle is a ferocious animal to an aphid, for she eats so many of them that she can soon clean up a colony. She eats other insects, too.

In fact, ladybirds are so valuable that farmers buy them by the pound when they can get them. Every summer, masses of them appear on the shrubbery in an area on Mount Lemmon, on Arizona's Coronado National Forest. Often they are collected and sold, under Forest Service permit, to farmers and orchardists.

The dragonfly that swoops and darts about so gracefully is feeding on gnats and mosquitoes as it flies. Honey bees not only make honey, but help to pollinate the flowers. All of these insects are often seen on the forests, around campgrounds, and in grassy, open woodlands.

The Alaska brown bear lives only in Alaska; the moose lives in most of the extreme northern states from Maine to Alaska, dipping south through Idaho and western Montana and Wyoming into northwestern Colorado and the Wasatch National

Deer on winter range. The plants are bitterbrush, an important winter feed for deer and elk.

Forest in Utah.

The mountain goat, like the bighorns, frequents the high peaks, and is even more sure-footed, if that is possible. He lives on some of the national forests of the Northern and Pacific Northwest regions and also in the national parks of those areas.

Elk live mostly in the Rocky Mountain and Pacific Coast states; white-tailed deer live on the forests of nearly all the states, though they are more an eastern deer than a western one. Mule deer are found throughout the West. An interesting big-game animal seen only in the West is the pronghorn antelope, which is not an antelope at all. It is in a family by itself and has no near relatives. This fleet-footed animal is much prized by big-game

Boy Scouts are learning to plant bitterbrush seedlings for future winter feed for deer and elk.

hunters. It likes sagebrush flats, and it roams the deserts of the Southwest as well as the flatter areas of the northern states.

Black bear (and brown, which is merely a color phase of the black) is on many of the national forests; the grizzly bear has largely been exterminated from all the states except Alaska, and is now in danger of extinction. It is generally confined to high mountains in a few western states.

Another carnivore that has been nearly exterminated by man and driven into remote wilderness areas is the mountain lion— also called puma, cougar, and panther in various sections of the country. This big cat has been persecuted by ranchers because they fear it will kill their stock, and by hunters because deer is its favorite food. However, many deer have starved to death because mountain lions and other predators were eliminated and the herds became too large for the available food supply. Two states—Florida and South Dakota—have laws against killing mountain lions, and a few others, such as Colorado, have declared it a big-game animal and have open and closed seasons; only Arizona still pays a bounty on it.

The timber, or gray, wolf has also been almost exterminated in the United States, except in Alaska. A few remain in the northern part of Michigan, Wisconsin, and Minnesota—including Superior National Forest and Isle Royale National Park, where they are protected by law.

Many of the smaller animals, such as beavers, foxes, skunks, and bobcats, can be seen on forests in all, or nearly all, of the states. Some other animals are in small areas only. For instance, the rare Chiricahua squirrel is found only in the Chiricahua Mountains on the Coronado National Forest, and most of the

A black bear released in the Muddy Creek Game Management Unit, on the Ouachita National Forest in Arkansas. Bear are being trapped in Michigan and Canada to restock the management area.

The Kaibab squirrel (left) and the Abert (right) are rare species with relatively limited ranges that do not overlap.

Arizona gray squirrels live on this forest.

The Kaibab squirrel is confined to the North Rim of the Grand Canyon National Park and the Kaibab National Forest on the north side of the Canyon. His relative, the Abert squirrel, roams the South Rim and parts of New Mexico, Colorado, and Utah.

These handsome tassel-eared squirrels, so-called because, except in summer, tufts of hair grow from the tips of their ears, are the most colorful of all our squirrels. The Kaibab has a black breast and dark sides and an all-white plume of a tail; the Abert has a gray tail that is white underneath, and a light breast. Because they are so rare, the Kaibab squirrel is protected from hunters, but there are usually open seasons on the Abert.

The red wolf has almost become extinct. It resembles a coyote, and many have been shot in the mistaken belief that they were coyotes. But it is slightly larger, and redder, and carries its tail up when it runs, whereas the coyote carries his down. At one time the red wolf could be seen from Texas and Oklahoma eastward to Florida and northward to Illinois and Indiana. Now it is hoped that a few may still be living in Texas, Louisiana, and Arkansas.

Red wolves are very shy and withdraw deep into the forest; so it is not easy to count them. But on the Ouachita National Forest, in Arkansas, an experiment is going on to determine whether red wolves are on the forest. A record was made of a red wolf's howl in Canada's Algonquin Provincial Park, and this record is played from time to time on the Ouachita Forest, in the hope that a red wolf will answer it.

Two interesting inhabitants of southern forests are the alligator, now threatened with extinction, and the armadillo, our only "armored" mammal. The armadillo, a tropical animal, entered Texas from Mexico, and then spread eastward to Florida and northward through Oklahoma and Arkansas. It is from fifteen to twenty inches long without the tail, which is almost as long; the body, top of the head, and the tail are covered with a bony material. Although armadillos are beneficial, because they feed largely on insects, and are completely harmless, they are persecuted by man. Many are killed by automobiles, some of them intentionally.

ANIMALS OF THE SOUTHWEST

Many kinds of interesting mammals and birds are found on the desert floor and in the foothills of the southwestern forests. The kit fox, smallest of the foxes, has the biggest ears. The javelina (or peccary) is a kind of wild pig, although it does not much resemble our domestic pigs. It is considered prize game by hunters, who are permitted to shoot it during open seasons. Four to five thousand are generally harvested annually.

The little ringtailed cat, which isn't a cat at all but is a distant relative of the raccoon, has come up from Mexico. It ranges across all the southwestern states, including Colorado and Utah, and up the coast through California to southern Oregon. The ringtail, with its big eyes and round ears, has a most appealing look, and is said to make a good pet. Its tail is as long as its head and body—about fifteen inches—and has alternate dark-brown and white rings on the entire length. The rest of the ringtail is light gray in color, and it weighs two to three pounds. It is largely nocturnal, hunting for its food at night.

Game birds on the southwestern forests include Gambel's quail and the scaled quail, mourning dove, whitewinged and bandtailed pigeons, and the king of all game birds—the wild turkey. This all-American bird inhabits every national-forest region in the nation except Alaska, but is not found in every forest. By far the greater numbers are in the Southern and Southwest regions—55,000 each in these two regions, out of a total of 162,000.

The javelina (or peccary) is a kind of wild pig, although it does not much resemble our domestic pigs. It is considered prize game by hunters, who are permitted to shoot it during open season.

The ringtailed cat, which isn't a cat at all.

IMPROVING WILDLIFE HABITAT

These are only a few of the animals for which the Forest Service must provide a place to live and which the state fish and game commissions must manage. For that's the way it works. The National Forest Service is responsible for the habitat—for protecting and improving the places where animals live—and the state commissions are responsible for the animals. These two agencies cooperate closely, because the state agencies control hunting and fishing, declare open and closed seasons, sell licenses, and regulate the number of game animals and fish that can be taken. So it is important for them to know about habitat—its condition, how many animals it will support, which localities have more game animals than the habitat will support and which have less.

Logging operations can be managed to improve wildlife habitat instead of destroying it. Foresters are learning a surprising fact—that a mature forest is usually not a good home for wildlife. Because sunshine cannot sift through the heavy crowns of the trees, there is little vegetation on the floor of such a forest, and the branches of the trees are too high to furnish browse for deer and elk. When the forest is thinned, sunshine reaches its floor, and vegetation soon starts growing and provides food for wildlife. If some of a forest is clear cut, grass and brush quickly follow, and feed is even better. Sometimes openings made by clear cutting are not reforested but are left to provide wildlife with lower-growing vegetation; and sometimes low-value timber is taken out to make a clearing for wildlife.

Logging roads no longer in use are often planted with grass and other vegetation for wildlife. Slash, which was once burned as soon as the logging was finished, now is sometimes left, except along roads and in high fire-hazard areas, for it provides food for browsing animals and shelter for smaller ones. "Den trees" and old "snags"—dead trees—containing holes where birds and small, tree-climbing animals make their homes, are left standing.

Sufficient winter forage for wildlife is not always easy to maintain. Where necessary, the Forest Service attempts to remove livestock from the deer and elks' winter range in time for the grass and other plants to start growing again. Research is being carried on in various sections to determine the best forage for all animals, domestic and wild. In Utah, for instance, experiments have developed superior strains of rubber rabbitbush, which grows rapidly and can be aerially seeded with grass and other plants to make good winter feed. Another important branch of research is the attempt to find ways to control insects and disease without using harmful insecticides and herbicides.

Water for wildlife is a major problem; here, again, the state and Forest Service cooperate closely. The Forest Service maintains the watersheds where the streams originate; it protects the trees and natural vegetation along the banks from being cut; and it constructs roads to minimize damage to the streams. The state keeps the streams stocked with fish, and sometimes, under a Forest Service special-use permit, builds lakes on the forests, stocking them with fish.

Occasionally that expert dam-builder and lumberman, the beaver, will "help" in these projects. A pair of these animals, looking for a good place to build their home, come to a stream in an opening where quakies grow and spread upward across a hillside. The beavers gnaw through the trunks of trees at the water's edge and drop them across the stream, making a dam, and soon the opening is a pond or lake.

The beavers build their house in the pond, using tree branches and brush and mud; the top of the house is above water, but the entrance is underwater. Here the beavers live and raise their family, feeding on willows and quakies and alders that they cut and drag to the pond. Other water animals come to the pond, and waterfowl build their nests along the edge. When anything happens to the dam, the beavers quickly mend or rebuild it.

Finally, they use up all the feed within reach of the pond; then they move on to another place, perhaps miles from the first one, and go through the cycle again. The first dam goes to pieces, the pond drains, and grass and shrubs grow again in an open meadow, offering good food for grazing wildlife.

Making water available to wildlife is not always an easy task, but the Forest Service works at it. Where streams or lakes are not within easy distance, foresters are making various kinds of watering places. Many of these are simply small ponds, perhaps a quarter acre in size, which are filled by rain or underground water where animals of all sizes can drink.

Various ingenious types of miniature watersheds—"trick tanks" or "guzzlers"—are being built, especially in areas where there is no water within a radius of a half mile or so. The trick tanks, particularly in the Kaibab Forest, are made of corrugated metal, which catches rain and channels it into large storage tanks. Water flows by gravity into the trough below the tank and is controlled by a protected float valve at one end. An escape ramp, formed of wire screen, at the other end of the trough permits birds and other small animals to drink without danger of being drowned.

The "quail guzzler," used in California, is a pit lined with concrete and covered over with an "apron" to collect the rain. The apron slants down to the bottom of the pit, forming a ramp, so that birds can get down to the water, but larger animals cannot.

The "riffle sifter" is a unique piece of machinery designed to take most of the silt out of the gravel beds where salmon spawn. Salmon live in salt water in the Pacific Ocean but spawn in freshwater streams. In the late summer or fall, they go far up the streams to "riffles"—gravel beds covered by a shallow, rapid flow of water. Here each female uses her tail to hollow out a hole, or "redd," in the gravel. Then she lays her eggs, sometimes as many as 8,000. A male fertilizes the eggs by covering them with a milky fluid called "milt"; finally, the fish cover the eggs with gravel.

The parents have eaten nothing since leaving salt water, and, having started the new generation on its way, they die.

The eggs hatch in early winter, but the young fish do not emerge from the gravel until spring, when they are about an inch long. Some species go immediately to salt water, but others remain in the streams for a year or more.

It is essential for water to circulate through the gravel to

It is hoped that a "riffle sifter," such as this one, will remove much of the silt from salmon-spawning gravels and greatly increase the productivity of salmon.

supply oxygen to the developing embryos in the eggs and to the newly hatched fish; the less silt in the gravel, the greater the chance for the young fish to survive. The Forest Service realized that if a device could be worked out to remove much of the silt from the gravel beds, the number of salmon available to commercial fishermen could be multiplied many times. So its Equipment Development Center in California went to work on the problem.

In conjunction with heavy-machinery manufacturing companies, the Center is experimenting with machines that plow and loosen the gravel and silt, vacuum or suck up the silt-laden water, and discharge it through a nozzle 100 feet beyond the bank. Such a machine must be used before the salmon begin to spawn.

SPECIAL CARE FOR ENDANGERED SPECIES

Red-carpet treatment, in the words of the Forest Service, is given to the rare and endangered species on the national forests. An example of this is the attention being given to the protection of the osprey, or fish hawk, on the Deschutes National Forest in Oregon. In June, 1969, the American Osprey Protection Area was established at the Crane Prairie Reservoir on the Deschutes Forest. This new management program is being carried out in cooperation with the Oregon Game Commission and the U.S. Bureau of Reclamation, which built the reservoir.

The Crane Prairie Reservoir is ideal for the ospreys' nesting purposes, because the lodgepole pine trees killed by rising water were left in place and the reservoir stocked with fish, which is the osprey's food. The ospreys come in the spring, lay two to four eggs in their ramshackle nests on the dead snags, and raise their young during the summer. Then they go south for the winter.

The Protection Area includes the reservoir and a 6,750-acre marginal strip around it, in which no hunting is allowed during nesting season. In a 1968 survey, the Forest Service found fifty nests, twenty-seven of which were being used by nesting birds, the largest concentration of nesting ospreys in the Pacific Northwest.

Numerous other rare and threatened species are given special attention. In cooperation with the National Audubon Society, a record is made of all bald-eagle nests in the national forests, and trees are left standing around each nest tree as a buffer zone.

In Michigan's Huron National Forest, the Forest Service is cooperating with the State of Michigan to provide nesting sites for the Kirtland's warblers. This choosy little bird won't nest anywhere but on the ground under a jack pine young enough to have branches close to the ground, which means that the pine must be six to twenty feet tall. When the pines grow so tall that the lower branches fall off and no longer cover the nests, the warblers move on to a younger thicket.

Unfortunately, the cones of the jack pine will open and scatter their seeds only under extreme heat, and forest fires have become very infrequent in Michigan. So young jack-pine thickets are becoming fewer and fewer. The Forest Service is attempting to solve this problem by setting aside a four-thousand-acre tract and, in a very carefully controlled project known as "Operation Pop-Cone," burning one-twelfth of it every five years, thereby insuring the warblers a continuing supply of young jack pine. The state has set aside an additional 2,700 acres for their small summer visitors.

A study of the habitat requirements of the masked bobwhite in Mexico has been made, so that the bird can be reintroduced on the Coronado National Forest in Arizona. The quail for this purpose are being raised in the Patuxent Wildlife Research Center of the Bureau of Sport Fisheries and Wildlife, in the Department of the Interior.

The largest soaring land bird in America, and one of the rarest of our endangered species, the California condor lives on a California national forest. At one time he ranged from Arizona and Utah west to California and north to the Columbia River in Oregon. Now the entire population, probably about fifty birds, lives almost entirely in two sanctuaries—the Sespe and the Sisquoc—on the Los Padres National Forest, north and northwest of Los Angeles.

The condor feeds entirely on carrion, and it is difficult to protect him because he ranges so far—forty to fifty miles—in search of it. However, five agencies are combining their efforts to save him: the National Audubon Society, the University of California, the Bureau of Sport Fisheries and Wildlife, California's Department of Fish and Game, and the National Forest Service.

So wildlife, one of the nation's important resources, is being maintained on the national forests, harvested by hunters and fishermen when necessary, but more often "shot" by photographers and enjoyed by millions of visitors to the campgrounds and recreation areas.

Chapter 7

FORESTS ARE FOR CAMPING

"Lady, will you put a worm on my hook?"

We looked up from our camp lunch at Caney Lakes, on Louisiana's Kisatchie National Forest, to see a small boy with a fishing pole and large hook in one hand and a tiny, badly mangled worm in the other. From the looks of it, he had been struggling for some time to put worm on hook; but worm was so little and hook so large that no one could have succeeded.

Neither could we resist that small, pleading face. We couldn't find a bigger worm; so we fixed him up with a piece of cheese on his hook. It took him less than two minutes to catch a fair-size fish with it—and happiness was Caney Lakes.

THE CAMPING EXPLOSION

We were camped in a small tent-trailer on the lower lake, in one of two large campgrounds on Caney Lakes. All around us we were seeing what is meant by "the camping explosion." There were people in every direction, in campers, in trailers, in tents. There were plenty of other little boys to keep our small fisherman company, and little girls, too.

Young people of all ages were enjoying the forest—swimming at the lower end of the lake off a fine beach complete with bathhouse; water skiing off a beach and boat ramps apart from the swimming; wading and fishing at the edge of the lake near us;

Canoers on one of the many lakes in the vast Boundary Waters Canoe Area.

or hiking the paths and "neighboring" with fellow campers. Not just "young" people, but people of all ages, were out in force. Parents of the children, and often *their* parents, were there. People of three generations might be camping in the same trailer —enjoying the outdoors, playing, resting, relaxing, or watching water-skiers whiz by on the lake.

Kisatchie, Louisiana's only national forest, is divided into eight somewhat widely separated sections, north and west of Alexandria. Caney Lakes is one of the three northernmost sections; it has some of the finest campgrounds in the national forests.

We had set up our trailer in a spacious campground where the forest is entirely man-made from an old cotton plantation, and the trees are in straight rows, wide enough apart to maneuver a trailer between them. The campsites, complete with stone fireplaces and picnic tables, are clean and inviting, and there is a pleasant view across the lake.

Having arrived about noon, we had our pick of campsites, but every site was taken by four o'clock. By nightfall, groups were sitting around campfires strumming banjos and guitars and singing; people strolled from camp to camp, getting acquainted and exchanging stories in the good fellowship that is a part of every camping experience. We enjoyed camping there so much that we stayed much longer than we had planned, and had trouble, finally, tearing ourselves away.

The primary work load of the Forest Service at Caney Lakes is recreation, and a five-year building and development program, costing about $750,000, is under way. More picnic areas will be added, and the campgrounds will be greatly enlarged, with electric outlets at the trailer sites. There will be separate areas for group camping and group picnicking, and several additional washrooms.

A new visitor center provides information and entertainment

for campers and other visitors to the forest; and an outdoor amphitheater, to be the setting for fireside talks, is in the planning stage, as are nature trails and more beaches, with bathhouses. This recreation complex is so carefully planned that it could serve as a model for other new recreation areas in the national forests, to help take care of more than fifty million people camping each year in public campgrounds.

But the other national forests are not waiting for models. For several years, their recreation areas have been undergoing a program of improvement and expansion, adding campgrounds with modern sanitary facilities, nature trails, and visitor centers for the convenience and enjoyment of the public. It is now possible for a family to travel across the United States and camp in a national forest or national grassland every night.

As of June 30, 1969, there were 5,197 campgrounds in the national forests, with room for 401,000 campers at one time. These range all the way from Diamond Lake, with room for 1,675—on Oregon's Umpqua National Forest—to tiny campgrounds for two, three, or four families, tucked away along the bank of a clear mountain stream or a quiet lake. In the larger campgrounds, naturalists are often on hand to tell visitors about the many activities in the forests.

The Redfish Lake Point Campground, at the north end of Redfish Lake, on Idaho's Sawtooth National Forest, is a research campground. Different kinds of grills—such as standup grills and fire circles—and other facilities are installed to find out what people like best. There are benches along the trail at the edge of the lake, and boat ramps, and, eventually, there will be 200 camping units.

An important expansion program is under way on Florida's Ocala National Forest, oldest national forest east of the Mississippi River. The recreation areas at Juniper Springs and Alexander Springs on Ocala are two of the best equipped in the

Forest Service, with tables, and group picnic shelters, tent-camping spaces, and trailer sites that have electric and sewer hookups.

New camping centers are being developed at other locations on the forest, which boasts more than 200 lakes and is in a lovely area of green, rolling hills. Two of the new centers are on Lake Dorr and Clearwater Lake; together they have seventy-seven campsites. These new sites are all engineered to accommodate self-contained trailers up to twenty-four feet in length. The Forest Service tells you that ten years ago most of the camping was tent camping, and so the sites were planned for tents. But today there are more trailers than tents, and the sites have to be arranged quite differently to provide easy access for trailers. To be fully convinced of that, try, just once, to back a trailer into an old-style site!

The Lake Dorr campsites all have outdoor fireplaces or fire rings for cooking, and tables with benches. Beaches and bathhouses and launching ramps make swimming and boating popular, and there are smooth, grassy picnic areas. Clean, modern sanitary facilities include showers.

Plans for Clearwater Lake call for seven camping loops, of which only two, offering forty-two spacious units, have been completed. The remaining five loops are waiting for more funds.

Ambitious as it is, the expansion of camping facilities on the Ocala Forest is not expected to keep pace with the demand for campsites. In Florida sunshine and with the fun of Florida water at hand, the camping explosion is evident here every month in the year.

CAMPING IS FOR FUN

Alexander Spring, Florida's thirteenth largest, flows eighty million gallons of water a day; Juniper flows eight-and-a-half million gallons a day. These crystal-clear springs provide natural swimming areas, and they, with others in the forest, supply water for numerous lakes and fishing streams—an unbeatable lure to campers.

One June afternoon, we set our trailer down early at Alexander Springs, because we knew the campground would fill up fast. By evening the place was running over with people, young and old, all bent on having fun. Some were hurrying to the big swimming beach at the Spring for a dip before supper; others were strolling along the nature trails. Tantalizing odors rose from camp grills where steaks were being broiled and coffee brewed.

Three little girls, brimming over with excitement, told us they had seen two armadillos and a turtle laying eggs and had fed a raccoon. A few minutes later, the raccoon himself ambled up, with an eye to more food, and we accommodated him with the scraps from our supper. Late that night he must have returned with a friend, because we heard garbage-can lids clanging in all directions and an occasional scuffle, when two raccoons apparently had designs on the same delicacy.

A canoe trip down beautiful Alexander Spring Creek was a high point of our visit to the forest. We floated down this wide, quiet river, between banks lined with flowers, shrubs, and trees, and remembered that this is the only national forest that has subtropical vegetation. Occasionally we had to push the canoe through floating gardens of spatterdock, water hyacinths, and tall, blue-flowered pickerel weed.

Many of the water plants were thickly encrusted with the pearly eggs of the green, or "apple," snail—so many that it was beyond belief—and the snails, too, were everywhere, in the water and out of it. These big fellows are the favorite food of the rare, subtropical limpkin. So of course we hoped to see some limpkins, in this place where their food is in such great supply—we had heard the river called "Limpkin Alley." And see them we did!

Singly and in twos and threes and flocks up to six and eight, they waded, long-legged, along the edge of the stream, picking off the snails and routing them out of their shells with long, curved bills.

Some took wing with loud, protesting squawks as our canoe approached; others moved back into the shadows, clucking and scolding, until we had passed. And once we heard the eerie wail for which this bird is famous.

Gaudily-colored wood ducks flew up from the water ahead of us. A mother hen on the bank fluttered along in a "broken-wing act," apparently trying to lure us away from a hidden nest. The shrill cry of an osprey came from a bird so high overhead that we could hardly see it; yet the call seemed close at hand.

We saw alligators lying along the banks, turtles sunning themselves on logs, and egrets and other herons. Our guide told us that he often saw otters playing in the water, and had we come in the early morning or late evening, we would probably have seen a white-tailed deer drinking at the water's edge. Ocala National Forest has the largest deer herd in the southeastern states.

At journey's end, we pulled the canoe up on a grassy bank and loaded it onto a truck that was waiting to take us back to camp. Before leaving, we ate a picnic lunch under a tree, and a pair of bobwhite quail came to look us over and daintily pick up crumbs.

Rental canoes are available at both Alexander Springs and Juniper Springs, and a paddlewheel boat, for a small fee, takes visitors on an hour's trip on the Alexander Spring Creek.

Although the flow from Juniper Spring is only four feet wide, it makes a lovely little stream that is popular with canoers. This area, too, teemed with people when we visited there, all having a good time.

The people in our campground came from all over the coun-

Tent camping at Juniper Springs.

try—from Maine, Michigan, Oregon, California. A steelworker from Indiana camped next to a silversmith from Massachusetts, and they compared notes on hand-crafting metals. An electrical engineer from New York told us how to hook up our extra trailer battery to our car generator, so that it would always be charged. A candle manufacturer was making a flying trip to California, staying overnight in national forests.

This is one of the factors back of the camping explosion: The chance to talk with people from everywhere and exchange ideas and experiences. Another factor is that camping offers a low-cost vacation in some of the loveliest parts of America.

Here the national forests shine. Almost always, the setting is superb, the fee for using the forest, if there is a fee, is very modest, and the campsites are comfortable and convenient. A camper doesn't need elaborate equipment to enjoy them; we once camped in Ocala in a rented tent—one that sets up with lightweight aluminum tubes, with no center pole or stakes. We set it up in ten

Raccoons often frequent national-forest campgrounds and are always ready to clean up the "leftovers."

minutes, and took it down in less than that, in a pouring rain, on our last day in camp. If we can do it, anyone can.

One evening, in our search for interesting places to camp, we pulled into the campground at Cedar Lake, in the western end of Ouachita National Forest, which spills over the line into Oklahoma from Arkansas. We had come over the beautiful Talimena Scenic Drive, from Mena, Arkansas, and had taken our time on the road. It was nearly dusk when we reached the campground. All the good sites on the north side of the lake were taken, but we found an excellent spot on the south side.

There was no electricity at the campsite, but we needed none; our trailer was lighted by an extra battery and our little cook stove was supplied with gas from a tank on the tongue of the trailer. We had finished supper and were lingering over coffee, when the forester on duty at night stopped by to tell us we were the only campers in the south campground. We weren't afraid, though, even if we were just a couple of women, for we felt as safe in this big forest as we did at home.

The forester told us about the wildlife that would be abroad at night; so we piled the dishes into a pan on the outdoor table and drove along the forest road to see what we could see. Sure enough, before we had gone very far, we had deer in the headlights of the car, and raccoons, owls, cottontail rabbits, and an opossum. The forester had said there were many foxes in the area, but, much to our disappointment, we didn't see any. Before we left for the ride, we had put out some grapes and a pear, because the forester said that foxes especially liked them. When we returned, the fruit was gone. So a fox was probably at our camp enjoying our fruit while we were out in the woods looking for him!

Campers having fun at Cedar Lake, on the Oklahoma side of Ouachita National Forest.

We left the dishwashing for daylight, and went to bed and to sleep—but not for long! Clatter! Bang! Clatter! Bang! It sounded as if our dishes were going in all directions. And that's just what was happening. We turned a flashlight on the table, and there was a big, fat raccoon, sitting on his haunches, with a knife in one front paw and plate in the other, waving the knife around as if he were just getting ready to butter a slice of bread.

He stared into the flashlight for a minute and then went unconcernedly back to the dishes. His system was to take a dish out of the pan, lick it off, and then hurl it to one side. Some of the dishes landed on the table and some on the ground. Fortunately, they were plastic; so they could take it. But finally, when he reached the platter, we decided that enough was enough, and went out to rescue the dishes. The raccoon withdrew into the shadows, but didn't go far. When we had gathered up the dishes

First snowfall at beautiful Lake Island, on Colorado's Grand Mesa National Forest.

and taken them inside, we put several slices of bread on the table, and he cleaned them up in short order.

The camping explosion is felt even on an 11,000-foot mountain. Western Colorado's Grand Mesa National Forest covers the mesa of the same name, which Coloradans brag is the largest flat-topped mountain in the world. We were surprised to find on top of this mesa some of the best campgrounds we had seen, with modern lighted washrooms; clean, spacious campsites; and firewood, cut and piled in bins, ready for the campers' use.

There are private lodges with cabins and trailer sites on the mesa, for Grand Mesa is one of the most popular recreation areas in Colorado. Because there are more than 300 lakes and reservoirs, fishing and boating are the order of the day, with skiing and snow mobiling in winter. Long and short hiking trails lead to breathtaking scenic views. A hard-surfaced highway goes to

the top of the mesa, and the Rim Drive Road, also hard-surfaced, leads to the visitor center at Lands End, where there is a spectacular view of the surrounding area for a hundred miles and more. Good gravel roads go to many of the lakes and campgrounds.

In addition to sites for family camping, many forests provide facilities for group camping, both for adults and young people. These camps range all the way from groups of buildings to a mere cluster of sites for tents or camper-trailers. Boy Scouts, Girl Scouts, 4-H clubs, and other youth organizations have camps in the forests under a special-use permit from the Forest Service.

Sometimes organizations, such as the Y.M.C.A., lease land from the Forest Service and make camps available to other groups. Three school districts in Pulaski County send underprivileged children to the Y.M.C.A. Camp in Ouachita National Forest, where they can learn about growing things. A kitchen and dining hall and other buildings are at this twenty-acre site on a stream and lake, with swimming beach, boat dock, and canoes. The week after we visited there, square dancers from all over the South were expected.

National-forest campgrounds are on a first-come, first-served basis; reservations cannot be made. A small fee per day is charged in some, while others are free.

The Forest Service generally prefers that people camp in developed campgrounds, and in some areas this is required. But as often as not, visitors may camp anywhere in the forest, and many of them do just that. There are some primitive campgrounds in areas that can be reached only by jeeps or packing. But backpackers hiking the wilderness areas usually make their own camps. Backpacking is becoming a major American sport, and many entire families are taking to the woods, even the smallest member with a pack on his back.

Backpacking family camping in the Pasayten Wilderness, on Washington's Okanogan National Forest.

Some visitors spend their whole vacation camping in the forests. A family can pitch its tent beside a quiet lake or a rushing trout stream, in a grove of spruce or poplar or in a flower-strewn meadow, on the floor of a desert or high up on the side of a mountain. There is no end to the things a camper can see and do in the national forests. The Forest Service asks only that he build a safe fire, make absolutely sure that it is out when he leaves, and clean up his campsite before departing.

Chapter 8

WILDERNESS

Lift, skim, dip, pull. Easy does it. Pull across the water at an easy pace, smoothly, delightfully. Glide across water 300 feet deep—blue, sparkling water, warmly sun-kissed, and surrounded, away off there ahead and on every side, by the tall, green forest of a primitive wilderness.

Four of us were in two canoes, two specks in the immense Quetico–Superior Canoe Country, and we were in the midst of an experience unmatched anywhere else in the world.

The Quetico-Superior straddles our Canadian border, and so lies in two nations. The northern half of it is most of Canada's great Quetico Provincial Park; the southern half is the fabulous Boundary Waters Canoe Area on Superior National Forest, in northern Minnesota. As a national wilderness, it is unmarked by human habitation, unpenetrated except by canoe.

Here is a network of glacial lakes so numerous that there seems to be almost more water than land. Roads go to it through the forests from such points on Lake Superior as Grand Marais and Tofte—the famous Gunflint Trail and Sawbill Trail. At the ends of the roads, and at Ely, nearest town, and at recently developed Crane Lake Recreation Area, "western gateway," are outfitters that supply anything and everything for a canoeing expedition, long or short. Also at Ely is the Voyageur Visitor Center, to acquaint the visitor with the Canoe Area and its surroundings and give him help in exploring it.

The sides and bottom of Linnville Gorge are lined with flowering plants—dogwood, mountain laurel, rhododendrons, azaleas of various hues—that form great masses of color during the spring and summer months.

There are many canoe routes, or "canoe trails"; the longest starts at Fort Charlotte at the end of the Grand Portage Trail on the Pigeon River and follows the Canadian border to International Falls. This is the historic "Voyageur's Highway" which, in the days of fur-trading, was used by Indians and traders to bring their wares to Lake Superior. Grand Portage National Monument, at the Lake Superior end of the Trail, has a fine museum telling the story of the "Highway."

All roads end at the border of the Boundary Waters Canoe Area. Here the visitor leaves his car and takes to his canoe. He loads his supplies and camp outfit into it, dips his paddle, and is off to cross lake after lake. If the lakes are separated by land, he portages, carrying his canoe on his shoulders across the land (from a few hundred yards to half a mile), while his partner carries the gear. Often more than one trip is necessary.

Do they go for a day? They take along a lunch and eat it at a campground on an island. Do they stay for several weeks? They take a lightweight but durable tent, sleeping bags, cooking gear, and a hearty supply of dehydrated and lightweight food, manufactured especially for their use. At night, they camp in one of the primitive Forest Service campgrounds, supplied with tables and fireplaces, however—usually only one or two sites, on island or mainland. In any case, they take along reliable maps and charts of their route.

People go out by couples in a single canoe, or by parties in several canoes. On Moose Lake is the Charles L. Sommers Wilderness Canoe Base, largest in the world, which is operated by the Boy Scouts of America. Explorer Scouts come to it from all over the country to take canoe trips into the wilderness. They go out in crews of ten, with an advisor who comes with them and a guide supplied by the base, which also furnishes all the necessities for a nine-day trip.

The boys select their own food, with the condition that they eat what they take. They must also stay within weight and bulk limits. But they often bake pies and cakes along the way, in a reflector oven that is part of the cooking gear. They select their own route and do the navigating, paddling, portaging, camp-making, and cooking. A crew of ten Scouts, with advisor and guide, goes in four canoes, three persons to a canoe.

We went for a day with an outfitter and his wife from Sawbill Lake. We traveled three big lakes, portaged twice, and cooked our lunch in an island campground. There were thousands of people in the Canoe Area that day, but it is so large and the people were so scattered that we saw only a few, and those at a distance. Only one other canoe came near us; a man in it needed help from our man to get a fishhook out of his hand.

We paddled from early in the morning until almost dark to make our circle trip, and we thought we had covered quite a lot of territory. But on a two-foot map of the Boundary Waters Canoe Area, you can put a quarter down over our route and cover it.

Yet from almost the first dip of the paddle, solitariness and high adventure were combined for us. There is nothing in the world like the feeling that comes to you, a mere dot in this far-flung primitive wilderness, as you discover you are master of your tiny craft and can send it across the water, anywhere you want to go.

You cross the middle of a quiet lake, water hundreds of feet deep beneath you. You skirt the land, gliding near forest and underbrush, where a rose-breasted grosbeak flits along, keeping pace, and the almost continual sweet call of the white-throated sparrows reminds you that thousands of these small birds are nesting here. Perhaps you see a black bear, a moose, a deer, a bobcat, a beaver.

This is wilderness, where there are no roads, where no motor breaks the quiet—no horns honking, no traffic, no danger of find-ing, come evening, that all the camping places are taken. Every sound, every motion, is part of the natural wilderness.

It was like this when the Voyageurs pushed their bark and

skin canoes westward, nearly 250 years ago. Hopefully, it will be like this for hundreds of years to come. When people have moved to the moon and to Mars, the Boundary Waters Canoe Area can still offer a fresh, thrilling experience in a wilderness on Earth.

Although the Boundary Waters Canoe Area is unique, there are many other wilderness areas in the national forests where there are no motor vehicles, no roads, and only the sound of the wind in the trees, the songs of birds, or the call of a wild animal to his mate. They range from Montana and Idaho's Selway-Bitterroot Wilderness of more than 1,200,000 acres to New Hampshire's Great Gulf, containing only 5,552 acres; and they are scattered all the way from New England to California.

Canoers preparing to portage around a waterfall in the Boundary Waters Canoe Area.

WHY WE HAVE WILDERNESS

Why wilderness? Because of people's need to get away for a time, if only in their thoughts, from the problems and pressures of civilization. Even people who cannot actually tread the trails of these remote areas have the comfort of knowing that there are some places in our nation whose streams will never be polluted with pesticides, whose air will never be contaminated with the fumes from the exhausts of millions of cars, whose scenery will never be bulldozed out of existence by the heavy machinery of speedway builders, and whose wildlife will never be crowded from its habitat.

Realizing this need, the Forest Service began setting aside wilderness areas in the mid-1920's, long before the 1964 Wilderness Bill was passed by Congress. The first area to be designated a wilderness was 500,000 acres in New Mexico's Mogollon Mountains, on the Gila National Forest. This was followed shortly afterward by the Superior Primitive Area, which later became the Boundary Waters Canoe Area.

One by one, other wildernesses were set aside, until finally there were fifty-four; thirty-four primitive areas were also set aside. Before each area was designated a wilderness, public hearings were held.

The Wilderness Law passed by Congress in 1964 says:

> In order to assure that an increasing population, accompanied by expanding settlement and growing mechanization, does not occupy and modify all areas within the United States and its possessions, leaving no lands designated for preservation and protection in their natural condition, it is hereby declared to be the policy of the Congress to secure for the American people of present and future generations the benefits of an enduring resource of wilderness. . . .

Every Forest Service wilderness is protected by this law, and six primitive areas were also designated wildernesses. Other primitive areas and areas in other public lands, principally in national parks and national wildlife refuges, are also being considered for wildernesses. In a designated wilderness, no lumbering is permitted, no roads, no vehicles, no commercial buildings or summer homes. Hunting and fishing, under state laws, are usually permitted, however.

A designated wilderness is given a name, in which the word "wilderness" usually appears. When it is used, it is written with a capital letter: Selway-Bitterroot Wilderness.

A region must be extra special to become a wilderness. Great Gulf Wilderness, on the White Mountain National Forest, is a narrow, steep-sided valley on the eastern flank of the Presidential Range. It is four miles long and one-and-a-half miles wide. Scooped out by an ancient glacier, Great Gulf is an outstanding scenic attraction. There are no roads into it and motor vehicles are not permitted, but the toll road up Mount Washington forms

Scooped out by an ancient glacier, Great Gulf Wilderness is an outstanding scenic attraction.

Girl Scouts backpacking into the Three Sisters Wilderness, in Oregon's Deschutes and Willamette national forests, where there are no highways, no vehicles, no commercial buildings, and no homes.

the south boundary. The scenery can also be viewed from State 16, south of Gorham.

Many trails, including the famed Appalachian Trail, wind through the wilderness, and the Appalachian Mountain Club's popular Madison Huts, supplying food and lodging, are on the north rim. The Club also maintains two "back-country" shelters with fireplaces, which are free to hikers on a first-come, first-served basis.

Because the early pioneers cut down the forests in the eastern United States to make way for farms and towns and cities, there is practically no national wilderness in that section of our country. Besides the Great Gulf, only two other small eastern national-forest areas are in the National Wilderness Preservation System—Linnville Gorge and the Shining Rock Wilderness, both on the Pisgah National Forest in North Carolina.

Linnville Gorge, 7,600 acres, is the deep, rugged canyon of

the Linnville River, and the trails are so steep and rough that they are a challenge to experienced hikers. The sides and bottom of the Gorge are lined with flowering plants—dogwood, mountain laurel, rhododendrons, azaleas of various hues—that form great masses of color during the spring and summer months. Auto roads lead to good viewing points overlooking the Gorge, at Table Rock Mountain on the east rim and Wiseman's View on the west rim.

Shining Rock Wilderness is a 13,000-acre tract in the Balsam Mountains, on the western section of the forest. Outstanding for its many flowering plants, it is named for a white quartz outcropping that shines in the sun.

WESTERN WILDERNESS

Most of the wildernesses are in the West, where they were protected by national forests and national parks before man had a chance to exploit them. Many of them are in rugged "high country," not easily reached by civilization.

Largest of these, the Selway-Bitterroot Wilderness, lies on four national forests—Bitterroot, Clearwater, Lolo and Nezperce—in Montana and Idaho. The Bitterroot Mountains, which the Wilderness straddles, form the boundary between the two states.

Selway-Bitterroot Wilderness has nearly every big-game animal found in the United States—elk, moose, white-tailed and mule deer, black bear, and mountain goats. It boasts one of the largest elk herds in the country, so large that state and Forest Service are hard put to keep some of the elk from starving to death in the winter months. Devastating fires swept through parts of the wilderness in 1910 and 1919 and again in 1934. The heavy brush that grew over the burned areas now furnishes fine summer feed for the elk, but deep snows in the winter make foraging difficult for these animals. So hunting, or "harvesting," the elk, is encouraged during the open season.

The Three Sisters peaks dominate the Three Sisters Wilderness. Scott Lake, in the foreground, is in Oregon's Willamette National Forest.

Bull elk, with a group of cow elk in the background. Selway-Bitterroot Wilderness, lying in four national forests, has one of the largest elk herds in the country.

The half-million-acre Teton Wilderness, lying between Yellowstone National Park on the north and Teton National Park on the south, is also noted for its big game—elk, moose, deer, black and grizzly bear, and bighorn sheep. Rare trumpeter swans are often seen on some of its lakes.

The Continental Divide crosses the Teton Wilderness and provides the setting for "Parting of the Waters," where Two-Ocean Creek divides and becomes Atlantic Creek and Pacific Creek. The waters of Atlantic Creek flow into the Atlantic watershed by way of the Yellowstone, Missouri, and Mississippi rivers; the waters of the Pacific Creek enter the Pacific Ocean through the Snake and Columbia rivers. This is the only known spot where such a division of a stream occurs.

Rocky, brushy, and rugged in character, Siskiyou National Forest's Kalmiopsis Wilderness, in southwestern Oregon, is of special interest to botanists, for it protects several extremely rare species of plants that are relics of the pre-Ice Age. One of these is *Kalmiopsis leachiana,* or rock rhododendron, oldest member of the heath family. It is a small shrub with a rosy-pink flower that looks somewhat like a miniature rhododendron. Another pre-Ice Age relic is the Brewer or weeping spruce, which is found only in a small area in the Siskiyou Mountains. It resembles Engelmann spruce, but its branchlets are very slender and drooping. Many other interesting plants are found in this wilderness.

Unfortunately, its harsh, rough terrain is not very inviting. Even the trails are so primitive that travel by horseback is not recommended. Visitors are warned never to travel alone and always to take snake-bite kits, for rattlesnakes are numerous. Poison oak is another hazard throughout the area.

HIGH COUNTRY WILDERNESS

Much more inviting to the average hiker or horseback rider are the Bridger Wilderness, in Wyoming, and the Bob Marshall Wilderness, in Montana. These are high-country wildernesses, where big game abounds and snowbanks last the year round.

The 383,300-acre Bridger Wilderness, on the Bridger National Forest, stretches along the west slopes of the high and rugged

Moose—a common sight in most of the northern wildernesses.

Wind River Mountains, and contains some of the most magnificent scenery in the Rocky Mountains. The Continental Divide follows the crest of the mountains and forms the north and east boundary of the wilderness.

Glacial lakes lie amid snowbanks at 11,000 feet; 13,000-foot peaks, and better, rise from perpetual ice fields. Fremont Peak—named for the famous explorer, John C. Frémont—at 13,730 feet is the second highest peak in Wyoming. Deep canyons, alpine meadows, and spring-fed mountain streams add to the scenic splendor.

Bridger Wilderness is popular with hikers because of short trails leading to many of the lakes, where the fishing is fine. Long trails, for the hardier hiker and the horseback rider, cross the wilderness in all directions. These trails are plainly shown on five sectional maps, which the Forest Service has published for the use of visitors to the wilderness.

Six major entrances are scattered along the hundred-mile western boundary, where maps, rules for wilderness travel, and registration facilities are available. Seven patrolmen are constantly at work, maintaining trails, checking campsites, putting out fires, and contacting visitors. Outfitters at the entrances furnish horses, tents, supplies, food, and guides if desired for pack trips.

The immense Bob Marshall Wilderness is another prime favorite with hikers and horseback riders alike. This wilderness, nearly a million acres in extent, lies on two national forests—the Flathead and the Lewis and Clark, in Montana. The elevation ranges from 4,000 feet along the valley floors to more than 9,000 on the Continental Divide, which bisects the wilderness and forms the boundary between the two forests.

Here, again, is spectacular country—lofty peaks, deep valleys, mountain streams and lakes, alpine meadows bright with wildflowers. Big-game and bird hunting, fishing, horseback riding, hiking along quiet trails, mountain climbing, and, in winter,

A trail rider in Bridger Wilderness, part of the Bridger National Forest in Wyoming.

skiing and snowshoeing are among the sports that beckon. Some of the many scenic attractions are the Chinese Wall, a 1,000-foot-high escarpment extending approximately twelve miles along the Continental Divide; Big Salmon Lake, largest in the wilderness; Sentinel Mountain, with plant and animal fossils; Bullet Nose Mountain and nearby ice caves.

Sixteen popular trips are listed on the wilderness map, and it will take you from three days to ten days to hike one of them. The Big Salmon Lake trip (seven days, seventy miles) starts at Holland Lake, southwest entry to the wilderness, and goes to Big Salmon Lake by way of Gordon Creek and the South Fork of the Flathead River, then back to Holland Lake via the Big Salmon River. Three one-day side trips go to the Flathead Alps, Bullet Nose Mountain, and Haystack Mountain at the Chinese Wall.

Several trails start at Benchmark, a southeast end-of-the-road entrance, where there are campgrounds and an airstrip open to the public. Here and at other entrances are outfitters and guides for pack trips.

WHO HIKES THE WILDERNESS?

Every year more and more people are taking hiking trips. Whole families, small fry and all, disappear into the wilderness for weeks at a time, each with his necessities in a pack on his back. They return, not only with harder muscles and stronger bodies, but with an inner strength and a deeper understanding of the wonders of Nature.

Before embarking on such a strenuous trip, however, the wise family hardens up by starting with shorter hikes. These "trial runs" also show what will be needed in the way of supplies and what should be left at home, and, too, just how big a pack each member of the family can carry easily. The amount, of course, depends on the size and strength of each individual. The recommended pack size for a woman is thirty pounds (maximum, thirty-five) and for a man, forty (maximum, fifty). One family, however, after backpacking for years, carries heavier loads. The father starts with fifty-one pounds and the older son with forty-eight; the mother and older daughter each carry thirty-eight

Mountain goats live in the high crags of many western wildernesses. This young goat is in Montana's Anaconda-Pintlar Wilderness.

pounds, and the two youngest children, a boy and a girl, carry twenty-six pounds each.

Based on long experience with the wilderness, the Forest Service has worked out a list of safety rules. These rules are available at points of entry into the wilderness, and the well-versed hiker follows them to the letter. Here are a few things to remember:

Never travel the wilderness alone, and be sure that the leader of your party has had wilderness experience.

Be sure to let the ranger at the point of entry know where you are going and when you expect to return.

Build a safe campfire and keep it small. Scrape away all burnable material so that the soil is bare on an area at least six feet in diameter, and be sure there are no exposed roots.

Put out your fire before you leave; pour water on the ashes and stir thoroughly, until every spark has been quenched. A fire that starts from one little spark can ruin vast areas in a wilderness.

Leave your camping area as you would like to find it. Burn all litter that you can, and carry out everything that won't burn. Empty tin cans are easier to carry if you flatten them.

To avoid getting lost, stay with your party. Don't let an interesting bird or other small animal lure you away through the trees, out of sight of your camp.

Chapter 9

TRAILS AND ROADS

We rode single file along the narrow trail through the forest, our brother ahead of us, leading the pack horse. All of us were singing lustily, "It Ain't Gonna Rain No More," although it had been raining steadily for the last ten miles. Our brother looked back over his shoulder and said with a grin, "It can't possibly rain 'no more' than it is now!"

But how little he knew. We rode out from under the shelter of the trees into an open meadow, and the clouds seemed to open and pour buckets of water on us. It went off our slickers in streams and down our necks wherever it could find an opening.

We had left our western Colorado ranch that morning in bright sunshine and embarked on our annual ten-day fishing trip on the Uncompahgre National Forest. We were heading for the Little Cimarron, where we knew the fishing would be good.

The trail had climbed steadily, past Courthouse Mountain and Chimney Rock, and over Owl Creek Pass before it leveled off. Finally the rain began to slacken, and it had almost stopped by the time we reached a grove of Colorado spruce where we had camped the summer before. The boughs on the spruce trees were so thick that little rain had penetrated them, and the ground under the trees was almost dry. The firewood that we had piled up for "the next campers" was still there. To our delight, we were the next campers, which was not really surprising, because

Saguaro cactus at the desert-shrub level, as seen from the road going up Mount Lemmon on the Coronado National Forest.

149

we were truly in high country, and few people came this way.

We soon had a fire going within the circle of rocks that had ringed our fire the year before, and supper cooked and eaten. We made our beds on spruce boughs, cut from a newly fallen tree. We had no tent, but slept in the open, where we could watch the stars and listen to the wind in the trees and to night animals as they came to life around us.

Many years later we retraced our way along the old, familiar route. But things had changed! The Forest Service had replaced the trail with a graveled road, wide enough for two cars to pass, and the journey that had taken us all day to make with horses now took less than an hour by car. The solitude was gone, too. We met a number of cars and saw numerous hunters, for the big-game season was open. Wildlife was still abundant. We were told that there were lots of deer and elk and some bear.

Small animals occasionally scurried across the road in front of our car, and we saw where some beavers had started a logging project. They had cut down several trees above the road and were dragging branches from them to a pond some distance below the road. We didn't see the beavers, but small branches scattered along a trail to the pond showed that work was in progress.

The Forest Service has built many roads like this one, often with short, easy trails going off from them, where visitors can see the life of the forest and the many things going on in it. Every effort is being made by landscape architects and engineers to blend the roads and trails into the landscape and maintain natural roadside beauty. State and U.S. highways often cross the forests, too, and bring to the motorist a suprising variety of things to see.

ROCKY MOUNTAIN SKYWAYS

Wide, paved U.S. 550, once a narrow graveled road, winds through the Uncompahgre Valley in western Colorado and crosses the San Juan Mountains in unbelievably spectacular scenery. The old mining town of Ouray, lying at the head of the valley, is partially surrounded by the Uncompahgre National Forest. Here starts that portion of U.S. 550 popularly known as the Million Dollar Highway. It twists and climbs through high mountains and deep gorges, often clinging to the steep side of a canyon where it has been cut into sheer rock walls. It crosses the San Juan Range at Red Mountain Pass and drops down the other side to Silverton, another old mining town. Almost all the way to Silverton, and beyond, on its way to Durango, the road travels through national forests.

Both Ouray and Silverton are popular with tourists. In a hollow above Ouray, known as the "Amphitheater," a Forest Service campground is crowded during the summer months. Silverton is the northern terminal of the narrow-gauge railroad that, in summer, makes daily trips from Durango and goes through breathtaking Animas Gorge, across part of the San Juan National Forest.

Montana's Beartooth Highway runs between Red Lodge and Cooke City and the northeast entrance to Yellowstone National Park. In five switchbacks within ten miles, the highway climbs from the valley floor at Red Lodge to an elevation, at Beartooth Pass, of nearly 11,000 feet. At each switchback, the road nearly doubles back on itself.

This is one of the nation's most beautiful drives. For much of its length, it follows the crest of the mountains, at heights of 10,000 feet or more. Dipping down into Wyoming and turning back into Montana, the road passes through three national forests —the Gallatin and Custer in Montana and the Shoshone in Wyoming—and goes between the Beartooth Primitive Area and the North Absaroka Wilderness.

Sometimes the highway goes through forests of Engelmann spruce, Douglas-fir, and other conifers; sometimes it rises above timberline to alpine meadows, bright with wildflowers. Now and then interesting rock formations—limestone palisades and basalt dikes—line the road. Glacial moraines are there, and cirque lakes hollowed out of rocky walls by glaciers; waterfalls, and buttes such as Beartooth Butte, with lovely Beartooth Lake at its foot. Some can be seen from the road, while short trails lead to others.

EARTHQUAKE ON THE MADISON RIVER

Just north of West Yellowstone, western entrance to Yellowstone National Park, is the incredible Madison River Canyon Earthquake Area, on Montana's Gallatin National Forest. On the night of August 17, 1959, several hundred vacationers camping along the Madison River or staying in resorts near Hebgen Lake were jarred from their sleep by the violet shocks of an earthquake that sent a huge mass of rocks and earth hurtling into the canyon.

The earthquake killed twenty-eight people, burying most of them under thousands of tons of rock; it injured many more. At dawn Forest Service and Air Force helicopters started taking out the injured. By evening, a way had been cleared by bulldozers so that the rest of the people could leave.

We had gone only a few miles on U.S. 287 from West Yellowstone, when we began to see evidence of this mighty upheaval. The earth had fractured and dropped in places from eight to twenty-one feet. This resulted in two immense scarps—steep rock walls—and a number of smaller ones. One of the large ones, the Red Canyon Fault Scarp, runs for about fourteen miles along the high ridge north of the highway.

We followed the highway along the north shore of Hebgen Lake, a large man-made lake formed by a dam on the Madison River. Frequent signs along the highway, with pull-offs for viewing, point to the havoc caused by the earthquake. It tilted the floor of the lake toward the north, so that the north shore was dropped under water; docks and boat launches along the south shore were left high and dry. The old roadbed was broken up in several places, and some of it had slipped into the water. Buildings had been swept into the lake; a few of them were still visible from a viewing point a short distance from the road.

Past Hebgen Dam, the road turns south and follows the west bank of Earthquake Lake. This lake was formed by the huge landslide that swept down the south side of the canyon with such force that some of it was carried up the north side. It filled the mouth of the canyon to depths of two hundred to four hundred feet, and the lake rapidly filled behind this slide.

Several hundred people took refuge from the water on a high knoll, now called "Refuge Point," and waited out a night of terror. Forest Service smokejumpers parachuted in at dawn and set up a first-aid station for the injured.

A glass-walled visitor center faces the slide, and a naturalist tells the story of the earthquake and explains some of the geological features. A huge boulder bears a plaque in memory of the people killed by the earthquake.

OLD TRAILS AND NEW

Between Lolo, Montana, and Kooskia, Idaho, the Lewis and Clark Highway (U.S. 12) follows the trail where the Lewis and Clark party made its tortuous way. It goes through two national forests, the Lolo and the Clearwater, and combines history with magnificent scenery.

U.S. Highway 12 crosses the state of Washington and joins the Olympic Peninsula, encircling the Olympic National Forest, famous for its lush rain forests and large herds of Roosevelt elk. A paved road leads from the highway to Lake Quinault and, nearby, to a nature trail through a typical rain forest in the Quinault Natural Area.

Oregon's national forests offer such a wide variety of scenic attractions that it is hard to decide which way to go. One can go west to the Pacific Coast and follow U.S. 101 south to the unique seashore forest, Siuslaw; or go east to Mount Hood and then south through forests that straddle the high Cascades and are full of strange volcanic formations.

Highest mountain in Oregon, at 11,245 feet, snow-capped Mount Hood is a shining landmark for Portland and the surrounding country. Glaciers clothe the highest slopes, and steam and gases come from openings, called fumaroles, showing that the ancient volcano that gave birth to this mighty mountain is not completely dead.

The Timberline Trail encircles the mountain and traverses much of the Mount Hood Wilderness. The Oregon Skyline Trail starts at the Columbia Gorge, passes west of Mount Hood and goes to Timberline Lodge, then meanders south through the forest to Willamette and Deschutes national forests. It is a seg-

Lava Butte, on Deschutes National Forest, was formed by volcanic eruption. There is a Forest Service lookout on top of the butte and a visitor center at the bottom.

A stone tree in Lava Cast Forest, Deschutes National Forest. Casts of trees like this one were formed when slow-moving lava surrounded the trees and then cooled.

ment of the Pacific Crest National Scenic Trail, which starts at the Canadian Border and follows high mountain crests to Mexico. This trail and the Appalachian Trail were the first two to be designated National Scenic Trails by Congress.

The lava country on Deschutes National Forest is a different world from Mount Hood. Fifteen million years ago, volcanic eruption began spreading vast lava flows over eastern Oregon, and the eruptions continued until about three thousand years ago. Glacier-clad volcanic peaks rise from the Cascade Range; below them are lava buttes, flows, cinder cones, craters, ice caves, and glacial lakes. Five U.S. and state highways cross the forest, and Forest Service roads and trails go to volcanic formations and to lakes.

COASTAL FORESTS

Over on the coast the picture changes again. Along Siuslaw National Forest's ocean shoreline, rocky cliffs alternate with gentle beaches, where surf fishing, clam digging, agate hunting, swimming, and hiking are always under way.

At Cape Perpetua a road turns off to Cape Perpetua Visitor Center, where the theme, "Forces of Nature," suggests "storm waves smashing rocky headlands, howling winter winds uprooting giant trees, the countless marine creatures competing for a place to live, and the unseen micro-organisms relentlessly turning fallen vegetation into soil." A short movie helps the visitor understand these forces at work along the Oregon Coast.

Trails lead to the top of the Cape for a good view up and down the coast, and to various other points of interest. We took the trail to a tidal pool, where our naturalist guide pointed out all sorts of fascinating marine life. Gorgeous purple sea urchins clung to rocks around the edge of the pool; comical little hermit crabs, with discarded snail shells on their backs, scuttled across the bottom of the pool. There were interesting starfish, and the dangerous sea anemones, which look like beautiful flowers but are really animals; their "petals" are deadly tentacles that sting their prey and paralyze it.

Stretching for fifty miles along the coast, from Heceta Beach south to Coos Bay, are the remarkable Oregon Dunes; thirty-three miles of them are on the forest. Hiking is popular in the Dunes, which are a mile and a half to two miles wide; several private resorts offer "dune-buggy" rides.

Far different from the Oregon coastline are the Alaskan coastal national forests. These two immense forests—Tongass, containing sixteen million acres, and Chugach, with about five million—occupy hundreds of islands, large and small, along the southern coast and extend high up the flanks of the ice-capped coastal mountains on the mainland.

Many long, narrow inlets, fiords, and bays penetrate deep into the land, and numerous glaciers move down from the mountain tops to the sea, where they break off in the form of icebergs.

Tongass National Forest, largest in the National Forest System, has eleven thousand miles of shoreline. It covers many islands and sweeps up mountains on the mainland, cut deeply by glaciers on their way to the sea.

Sparkling waterfalls spill from "hanging lakes" left high on the mountainsides by the glaciers.

Tongass National Forest lies in the extreme southeastern section of Alaska and surrounds several important Alaskan cities, including Ketchikan, Wrangel, Petersburg, Sitka, and Juneau, the state capital. Haines and Skagway are at the northern tip.

The highway system in this forest is unique. It's marine! Until the state instituted its Marine Highway System through southeastern Alaska's Inside Passage, which goes into the heart of the Tongass Forest, it was practically inaccessible to the average traveler. Now three large auto ferries link the small communities that are the gateways to various parts of the forest. Campgrounds and picnic sites near the communities can be reached by car, and the more remote wilderness areas, by chartered plane or boat.

FOREST GLACIERS

From Juneau, a highway goes north to famed Mendenhall Glacier, about thirteen miles away. Here, around Mendenhall Lake, is the Mendenhall Glacier Recreation Area, with campground, picnic sites, and nature trails. The handsome, glass-walled visitor center, first to be built by the Forest Service, affords a spectacular view of the glacier, and naturalists are on hand to tell its story. This glacier and numerous others flow from a hundred-mile-long ice field on the summit of a high mountain range.

The totem poles of southeastern Alaska were carved by Indians and erected in front of their homes years ago. Whenever the Indians abandoned a village site, they left the totem poles standing. In the early 1940's the Forest Service collected and restored many of them, setting them up in totem-pole parks in more accessible places.

The Chugach National Forest, which encircles Prince William Sound and occupies Afognak Island, is reached by highways and a railroad. The Afognak segment is directly across the Shelikof Strait from Katmai National Monument, containing the Katmai Volcano and the Valley of Ten Thousand Smokes.

In both forests, the Forest Service maintains camp and picnic grounds; it has built and is maintaining over 160 cabins at good hunting and fishing spots on numerous lakes and bays.

Washington and California boast glaciers, too. The Glacier Peak Wilderness, in Washington's Mount Baker and Wenatchee national forests, has more than ninety glaciers on Glacier Peak and the many other peaks and ridges in the wilderness.

California's glaciers are in the high Sierras. In Inyo National Forest, Palisades Glacier is believed to hold the southernmost

Whenever the Indians of southeastern Alaska abandoned a village site, they left the totem poles they had carved and erected in front of their homes. In the early 1940's, the Forest Service collected and restored many of them, setting them up in totem-pole parks.

active glaciers in the United States. Inyo, in an alpine setting, has many other natural attractions: the Minarets, a jagged range of granite peaks; the Indiana Summit Natural Area, preserving a stand of virgin Jeffrey pines; Hot Creek, which starts as a cold-water stream and is warmed as it passes through an area of hot springs and fumaroles; the ancient bristlecone pines.

PROFILE OF A STREAM

Beautiful Lake Tahoe is surrounded on three sides by Eldorado and Tahoe national forests. At the south end of the lake, reached by U.S. Highway 50, is an interesting visitor center built on the bank of Taylor Creek. It has a "stream profile" chamber with a glass wall against the creek, below the level of the ground, so that the stream can be seen in profile. No privacy for stream dwellers here! Visitors can see into the water, into the soil of the bank, and the bank above ground, and watch living things of these zones in their natural surroundings —fish eggs and frog eggs hatching, dragonfly nymphs and caddis cases, salmon spawning, and all other life of the stream and bank.

A FLAMING CANYON

Nevada and Utah national forests hold a wealth of interesting and beautiful spots on good roads, ranging from snow-capped mountain ranges to unbelievable desert rock formations. One of these beauty spots is Flaming Gorge and adjoining canyons, now the lower end of an immense, man-made lake in the Uinta Mountains.

A Bureau of Reclamation dam near Dutch John, Utah, on the Ashley National Forest, has backed up the waters of the mighty Green River into a ninety-mile reservoir that extends almost to Green River, Wyoming. A national recreation area, managed as part of the Ashley National Forest, surrounds the lake, with boat ramps, fine campgrounds and picnic sites, and all the water sports—fishing, boating, water skiing, and swimming.

We zipped up the lake in a power boat, between the closely crowding, multicolored rock walls of Red Canyon, on through Hideout Canyon, with its modern campground that can be

A trail leads to the top of Cape Perpetua for this view of the forest and the coast and the visitor center, on Siuslaw National Forest.

reached only by boat, and through Kingfish and Horseshoe canyons. At last we came to the climax of the trip—Flaming Gorge itself, where glowing red rock walls rose high above us.

Red-walled canyons are almost a hallmark of the Flaming Gorge area. At the Red Canyon Visitor Center, we stood inside glass walls at the very edge, and caught our breath as we looked into the canyon and the water below. Outstanding exhibits in the center depict the various aspects of the forest, including wildlife and plant life. The wildflower exhibit is actual plants that have been carefully preserved.

We ended our visit to Flaming Gorge by taking the "Drive

through the Ages," an auto tour through Sheep Creek Canyon, where signs along the way point out the various geological formations. Fossils of marine animals show that this area was once covered by a sea.

THE SOUTHWEST—TODAY AND YESTERDAY

National forests of the Southwest rise from burning deserts to high, cool mountains. Here is a fantastically beautiful land, with brightly colored buttes and mesas and canyons deeply carved by wind and water. Here, too, are crumbling pueblos and cliff-dwelling ruins left by prehistoric Indians; here are trails of the Spanish explorers, ghost towns, and the remains of old mines and mills.

A few miles northeast of Tucson is a delightful place called Sabino Canyon. It is near Mount Lemmon, on the Coronado National Forest. A road goes up the canyon for three miles, crossing back and forth over Sabino Creek nine times on picturesque but very narrow bridges.

A visitor center at the mouth of the canyon has picnic grounds and a nice campground, a self-guiding half-mile nature trail through typical desert vegetation, and interesting exhibits characteristic of the area. Best of all, it has a movie that shows the various climatic zones and their accompanying zones of vegetation on Mount Lemmon, as this mountain rises abruptly from the desert to 9,250 feet.

In general, the movie follows the course of the scenic highway that climbs, by switchbacks, to the summit of the mountain, highest peak in the Santa Catalinas. On this drive, the visitor travels through climate and vegetation changes comparable to a trip to Canada from the Mexican Sonoran Desert. The drive starts at the desert-shrub level, where the annual rainfall is eleven inches; goes through the semidesert grassland, woodland, and chaparral at 4,500 feet; ponderosa pine forests between 6,200 and 7,200 feet; and mixed conifers, including alpine fir, at the highest levels, where total precipitation is thirty-three inches.

In New Mexico's Lincoln National Forest, a forest fire raged through the Capitan Mountains in May, 1950. Near Capitan Pass a bear cub, badly burned, was found clinging to a charred tree. This little bear was to become the living Smokey, used on posters and in Forest Service literature to caution against forest fires.

Smokey's burns were doctored, and after they healed, he was flown to the National Zoo in Washington, D.C., where he poses for "Smokey" posters. The people in the town of Capitan have built a log museum to commemorate him.

But the national forests of New Mexico don't stop with Smokey as a conversation piece. On the Carson National Forest is a talking beaver! "Hello! Welcome to Beaver National Forest," he will tell you in English and Spanish. Beaver National Forest, on U.S. Highway 84, is just one and a quarter acres in size.

Everything in this miniature forest is man-made, including the talking beaver. When a visitor presses a button, the beaver tells about the multiple-use program of the National Forest Service. There are other man-made animals—cattle, sheep, deer, and wild turkeys, as well as people, all half size. A family is having a picnic at a little table; a fisherman is on the bank of a tiny stream; two lumberjacks are about to cut down a tree; a fire lookout stands on the balcony of a fire tower.

The land for this little forest was leased to the Forest Service by the Charles Lathrop Pack Forestry Foundation, which has the nearby Ghost Ranch Museum. Here, close to Beaver Forest, are live animals, including mountain lions, bears, deer, and, in the Beaver House, a unique display of live beavers and illustrated exhibits that tell the history of the beaver in America. Other exhibits trace the geologic history of the area; telescopes are focused on the different strata in neighboring cliffs and buttes.

EASTERN ROADS AND TRAILS

Good roads and hiking trails to scenic and interesting places are as much a feature of eastern forests as western. In Vermont, the Long Trail, constructed by the Green Mountain Club, winds from the Canadian Border to the Massachusetts line; it follows the crest of the Green Mountains for eighty miles through the Green Mountain National Forest. At frequent intervals, the Club and the Forest Service have built cabins and other shelters, free to hikers. At Sherburne Pass, the Appalachian Trail joins the Long Trail and follows it to the Massachusetts line.

The famed Appalachian Trail stretches along the crest of the

At Roan Mountain, on the line between Pisgah and Cherokee national forests in Tennessee, the rhododendrons were at their best—clump after clump of dazzling color, as far as eye could see.

Appalachian Mountains for more than 2,000 miles, from Mount Katahdin in Maine to Springer Mountain in Georgia. Constructed and maintained by the various hiking clubs that make up the Appalachian Trail Conference, it goes through fourteen states, eight national forests, and two national parks. It is well marked and well constructed, beaten smooth in places by the feet of many hikers. Along the way are cabins and other shelters. Occasionally the Trail crosses highways where the motorist may park his car and take short hikes along it.

The beautiful Blue Ridge Parkway, a star of scenic highways, starts at Shenandoah National Park, in Virginia, crosses Pisgah National Forest, and enters Great Smoky Mountains National Park through the Cherokee Indian Reservation.

We traveled the Parkway in late June, and began seeing "purple" rhododendron (really a dark, lovely rose color) soon after we entered the Pisgah Forest. The farther southwest we went, the more beautiful the rhododendrons became, often growing in large masses. On Roan Mountain, twenty miles off the Parkway, on the line between Pisgah Forest and Cherokee National Forest in Tennessee, they were at their best—clump after clump of dazzling color, as far as the eye could see.

MEMORIAL TO A POET

At the Cherokee Indian Reservation, we turned southwest to Nantahala National Forest and the Joyce Kilmer Memorial Forest. The Memorial Forest, near Santeetlah Lake, is one of the wonders of the National Forest System. In 1934, the Veterans of Foreign Wars petitioned the U.S. Government to set aside a stand of trees as a memorial to the poet, Joyce Kilmer, who was killed in action in World War I.

The Forest Service studied millions of acres of forests all over the country before it finally decided upon this site, in the heart of Nantahala. Here is an area of 3,600 acres containing one of the few stands of virgin hardwood in our nation. These trees were growing before Columbus, or the Vikings, discovered the New World. They are, indeed, a fitting memorial to the poet who is immortalized by his poem "Trees."

Plaque Trail leads from the parking area into Poplar Cove, where huge hemlocks and tulip-poplar trees, hundreds of years old, tower into the sky. Here, too, are sycamore, basswood, beech, oak, and many other species of trees. On the trail is a plaque containing the poem "Trees," and in the heart of the cove, on a large boulder at the foot of a great hemlock, is a memorial inscription to the poet.

LONGBOWS AND FLOAT TRIPS

There are thousands of miles of other trails and roads in the national forests, so many that it would take several books to tell about all of them. In Kentucky's Daniel Boone National Forest, noted for its natural arches and other scenic features, is the Red River Gorge Drive. North of the Drive is the 7,000-acre Primitive Weapons Hunting Area, where hunters who enjoy using

Stretching for fifty miles along the coast, from Heceta Beach south to Coos Bay, are the remarkable Oregon Dunes; thirty-three miles of them are on the Siuslaw National Forest.

Canyon Rim overlook near Red Canyon Visitor Center.

primitive weapons have a field day, because only crossbows, longbows, cap-and-ball and muzzle-loading rifles are allowed in the area.

The Ozarks, in southwestern Missouri and northwestern Arkansas, are also famous for the beauty of their scenery. High cliffs and deep canyons, brilliantly colored caves and sparkling waterfalls, crystal-clear springs and lakes, most of them man-made, are among the things to see.

Float trips are popular in the Ozarks. The majority of "floaters" go to fish—trout in the White River, small-mouth bass in the Buffalo; small-mouth bass, large-mouth bass, and bream in the Mulberry. But many people go just to relax and enjoy the scenery along the way. You can float for half a day or for two weeks, but, unless you are an experienced river man, it's well to take along a professional guide.

Down on the Ouachita National Forest, the Ouachita River can be floated for forty-five miles, from the old Pine Ridge bridge to Lake Ouachita. Numerous access roads and landings are clearly marked, and mileage signs along the river tell boaters the distance to downstream landings. So the floater can select the length of trip he wants, and then sit back and relax while the current carries his boat through the forest along a different kind of "road."

Chapter 10

FUN IN WINTER

We were late and had to run to get on the last coach in the last hour of the last day of the summer season—a coach on the Jackson Hole aerial tramway to the top of Rendezvous Peak. Soon we were swinging on a cable above treetops and rocky mountainside; swinging, and climbing, up, up, up.

Below us, in an ever-widening vista, was fabled Jackson Hole, Wyoming, town and valley at the foot of the Grand Teton Mountain Range. On either side were other Teton peaks—Ship's Prow, Cody, and many more. To the top of Rendezvous, it's two and a half miles on the tram; from sea level, it's 10,446 feet straight up. Either way, Rendezvous and its range are part of the most rugged mountain country in the nation.

Just beneath us we saw two moose, lying down in a little open space between trees, taking their ease and paying no attention to the big coach that moved past over their heads. We—and sixty other passengers—could not get enough of watching them, and the mountainsides, and the valley.

Snow would fly here soon—in fact, we met it a few days later as we traveled on north. It would cover ridges and valleys and "bowls" with a thick, white blanket, a fun blanket. To these slopes of pure, dry snow, the skiers come in thousands. They ride up on the tram and on several kinds of chair lifts, and find spread below them miles of inviting, rolling, white speedways.

Skier sails off cornice of snow at Hoodoo Ski Bowl. Mount Washington and Three Sisters peaks in the background.

They go whizzing down ski trails that are mapped and marked, over such interesting-sounding terrain as Hoback and Sublette ridges and Cheyenne and Sheridan bowls. There are trails and slopes for every kind of skier, beginner to expert, over many square miles of mountainside.

A SPECIAL USE

Nearly all of this is on Teton National Forest, just south of Grand Teton National Park. The tramway runs over the forest; the ski runs are on it. The lower terminal of the tram is on land owned by the ski corporation that built the tram. This company also owns a skiers' base surrounding the terminal, the new Teton Village—a complex of lodges, restaurants, and shops.

Here, then, is still another use of the national forest. The company operating the tramway has a special-use permit for the ski area, which includes the tramway, chair lifts, and all facilities on national forest land. They charge skiers to ride or use the facilities they have provided. They also profit in spring, summer, and fall from sightseers (which we were), who come in even greater numbers than skiers.

There are many installations like this in the national forests. We rode another one, up New Mexico's Sandia Peak on Cibola National Forest. This time it was bighorn sheep below us on the rocky mountainside; and the pilot of the coach told us he had recently carried a bear in the coach, from the outskirts of Albuquerque to one of the mountain towers on the tramway, and released it there.

This time it was Albuquerque we saw, spread far up and down along a wide, flat desert valley. From the shelter at the top landing and from a mountaintop restaurant, we watched brilliant sunset, purple hills at dusk, and a dazzling blanket of city lights that met the stars.

We marveled at the installation of the two towers for the

Coach on Jackson Hole Tramway headed for the top.

cables, in places that seemed completely impossible. The pilot told us that every piece of steel and other materials that went into constructing one of the towers, and every man who worked on it, was taken to the site by helicopter. There was—and is, to-day—no other way to reach it.

Again we had to imagine the snow for winter sports, but we could well understand what brings so many people here year-round. This part of Cibola Forest is designated the Sandia Recreation Area. It has numerous trails, short and long, for hikers and horseback riders; some of the hikes are led by Forest Service naturalists. These include a winter snowshoe hike to the top of the peak, where snow lies six to seven feet deep in the winter months; the hikers ride back down on the tramway.

Sandia Peak is the focal point for most of the activities. Trails, tramway, and a scenic drive, the Sandia Crest Loop, climb from 4,900 feet to 10,678, through climatic zones and vegetation ranging from desert shrubs to alpine firs. Just off the drive is the Sandia Man Cave, where relics were found that were left by human hunters more than 20,000 years ago. The winter-sports area is served by a 7,500-foot chair lift and other lifts on the east side of the mountain, as well as by the tram, and the skiers rank from beginners to experts.

SNOW RANGERS ON THE JOB

The company operating the skiing facilities is responsible for skier safety, snow safety, and all ski-area activities. However, the Forest Service does not give up responsibility for the safety of its visitors. Here the "snow rangers" are in evidence. They maintain close inspection of all equipment, such as the tramways and lifts, and check the safety of ski slopes. They work with ski operators, and with state road departments to keep roads open in winter. Public safety is their first concern, and they are ready to help the visitor with any problem that arises. They keep a constant watch for signs of an avalanche, and if they decide that a ski trail is not safe for that day's run, they post it with warning signs.

In some areas in Colorado and Utah, snow rangers shoot down avalanches, if necessary, with 75 mm. recoilless guns or TNT. This must be done early in the morning, before skiing begins. Often the boom of the snow ranger's gun echoing in the valley serves as the alarm clock for skiers staying at nearby lodges.

Whether or not you ride a tramway over a national forest, the Forest Service is still your first hold on safety. A snow ranger, in his green jacket, with a bright yellow shoulder patch, is never very far away.

Other winter sports, too—snowshoeing, skating, tobogganing —are often a part of the fun in a ski area; newest is snowmobiling, a sport that is taking the country by storm. Snowmobiles—"snow buggies"—are motorized, streamlined, and on runners. They can go wherever there is snow, and are a fine substitute for skiing.

Snow ranger on duty at the Arizona Snow Bowl.

Probably because the sport is new, snowmobiling can mean trouble for the snow rangers. Some snowmobilers like to go where they shouldn't; some thoughtless ones enjoy chasing and harassing deer and other wildlife. But clubs are being formed,

snow trails are being developed for the snowmobiler, and regu-
lations are being worked out for their use, to minimize some of
the problems. The Western Snowmobile Association is made up
of many local clubs in the western mountains; they hold an annual
rally in March at West Yellowstone, Montana, in which there
are races, jumping contests, and tours to many points of interest.

WINTER SPORTS ARE BOOMING

There are approximately two hundred winter-sports areas on
the national forests, serving more than 350,000 persons at one
time. Nearly every forest that has snow also has at least one
winter-sports complex, and some of them have several. California
alone has forty-two, accommodating nearly 92,000 persons a
day.

The Presidential Range on the White Mountain National
Forest, which straddles the boundary between New Hampshire
and Maine, saw the pioneering of winter sports and is inter-
nationally known. Here Tuckerman Ravine, a glacial cirque on
the east slope of Mount Washington, is a true alpine ski area,
where the sport often lasts until mid-June. A cog railway takes
visitors up Mount Washington, and good trails lead from several
directions to the top; there is a toll road to the top, for motorists.
Wildcat Mountain is another winter-sports area on this forest,
at scenic Pinkham Notch; and there are still others here and on
Vermont's Green Mountain National Forest.

Lookout Mountain on Superior National Forest near Virginia,
Minnesota, is a leading area in the midwest. West of the Mississippi River, you can name almost any national forest and find
a winter-sports development on it. Sun Valley, on Idaho's Sawtooth Forest, near Ketchum, is world famous. Sun Valley Village
is outside the forest boundary, but many of the best ski runs are
on the forest. Nearly three miles of ski lifts located on Bald
Mountain take skiers to the runs. There are also many miles of

Gondolas pass on the tramway at the Sierra Blanca Ski Area.

ski trails, for ski tours, meandering through the mountains. Famous, too, are the ski areas on White River National Forest encircling Aspen, Colorado. Newest here is the Snowmass area west of Aspen.

New areas are opening every year; one in the Southwest is the Sierra Blanca, on the Lincoln National Forest in New Mexico, near Ruidoso. Here gondola cars travel up the mountainside on a tramway to an elevation of 11,400 feet, and an attractive ski lodge serves visitors around the year. This ski area is operated under a Forest Service permit by the Mescalero Apache Indians, whose reservation is directly south of this section of the forest.

You can get magnificent views of Mount Rainier and other peaks in the Cascade Range from Crystal Mountain's chair lifts and from the Mountain Top Restaurant, which is reached by chair lift. This winter-sports area is on Snoqualmie National Forest, at the edge of Mount Rainier National Park. It is one of nineteen ski areas located entirely on a national forest, operating under a special-use permit.

The facilities of the Hoodoo Ski Bowl, near Santiam Pass on Oregon's Deschutes National Forest, narrowly escaped being burned in the summer of 1967, the "Fire Year." A fire caused by lightning swept over 7,700 acres on the Willamette and Deschutes

Famed Timberline Lodge on Mount Hood.

forests and threatened the lodge and other base facilities, but the firefighters managed to save them with backfire and other action. Several wooden towers of a chair lift were destroyed, but two newer chair lifts with steel towers escaped much damage.

After the fire, the Forest Service and area management worked quickly to remove the downed trees and ground debris from the ski slopes and seed them with grass from helicopters. When winter came and the skiers returned, snow had covered the unsightly burn, and the Ski Bowl was back in business.

TIMBERLINE LODGE

One-of-a-kind is famous Timberline Lodge on the south slope of Oregon's Mount Hood, on Mount Hood National Forest. Timberline Lodge is owned by the Forest Service, but is leased

for management to a commercial company under a special-use permit. At a 6,000-foot altitude, it centers the fun on Mount Hood, where "winter" sports go on year-round. Skiing is popular in the summer months, because perpetual snow lies on the higher slopes.

The lodge operates two "sno-cats"—busses that take skiers and sightseers to the 10,000-foot level on the mountain. A bus up the side of a snow-covered mountain? But these busses are unique. They are mounted on big caterpillar treads that travel across snowbanks more easily than a sled could do it, carrying twenty passengers to a load. These offer skiers one of the longest ski runs in the country, from the 10,000-foot level to Government Camp, a small community several miles below the lodge, where there are also skiing facilities.

Timberline Lodge itself is unique. It was built by a federal agency during the dark days of the 1930's depression, to create

Bighorn rams hunting for feed on their winter range.

jobs. Many fine craftsmen, out of work, helped build it, carpenters, metalworkers, artists, woodcarvers combined to turn out a fabulous production. The four-story building is made entirely from Oregon wood and stone, and the furniture and interior decorations—paintings, carvings, iron work—are handmade.

Three motifs are used: pioneer, Indian, and Oregon wildlife. The carved newel posts of the stairway, made of old telephone poles, depict animals typical of the Northwest; a life-size carving of a mountain lion hangs over the lobby doorway. Redwood panels show pioneers on their way west. Floors are of beautiful Oregon oak, each board held in place by wooden pegs.

Millions of people are served through special-use permits such as these, which take them into places they would otherwise be unable to reach. These installations are the key to the tremendous growth of winter sports, providing not only a lift to the top of the ski runs, but food and shelter and a center for many activities.

On Grand Mesa, Colorado, for example, an area far removed from any large population center, foresters recorded more than 30,000 skiers in a recent winter—plus more than 10,000 who were there for "snow play" (as the foresters put it), most of them with snowcraft of some kind. This was a substantial increase over the year before, and most of the increase was in nonskiers—people who were encouraged by the presence of a recreation center, and roads kept open to it, to get out and enjoy the snowy forest.

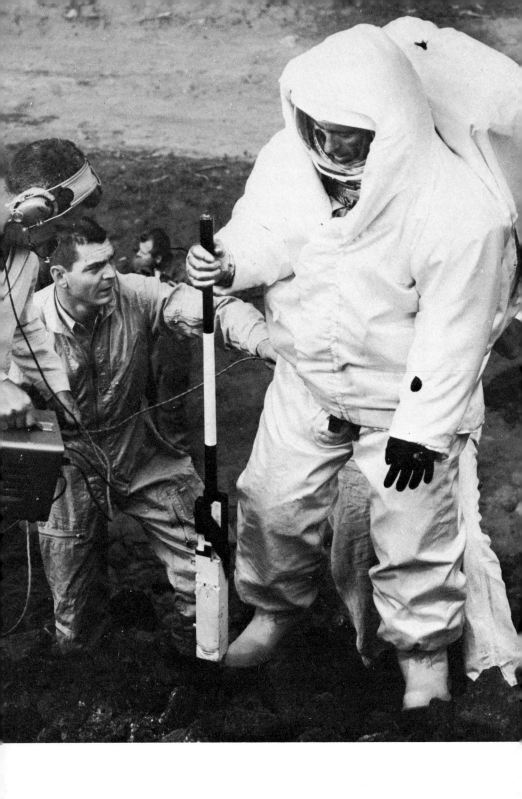

Chapter 11

LANDS OF MANY USES

Cattle moved down the road ahead of us, bawling. We inched our car and trailer through them, but we could not make much headway, because they were going the same way we were. Now and then one of them would dart across the road, and our slow progress would come to a sharp stop. Cattle bawled far ahead of us, and on either side, and far back of us. They spread upward along the hillside; we could hear them bawling in the ravine between us and the mountain, where we couldn't see them. We crept along for miles, often feeling the push of cattle against the car and against the trailer.

It was the day before the deer season opened, and the ranchers were getting their cattle down from the range. Much of the range was inside national-forest boundaries, and the deer hunters' use of the forests would begin the next day. Hunting and cattle often do not mix well. Thoughtless hunters leave gates open, and a rider then must spend a day or a week rounding up the cattle that, somehow or other, can always find an open gate. And a hunter, in heavy brush or in the failing light of dusk or sometimes just in excitement, cannot always tell a cow from a deer.

So ranchers like to get their cattle off the range before the hunting season starts. We could see various brands on the cattle near us—the Lazy A, the Circle Bar, the Rocking S. That meant

In the "lava lands" of Willamette National Forest, Oregon, astronaut Walter Cunningham tests his ability to climb on lava while dressed in a heavy space suit.

181

Just before the big-game hunting season opens, cattle being moved from the national forests clog the roads. When they entered the forest, a forester counted them in; when they leave, a forester counts them out.

that several ranches were cooperating to round up the cattle and move them from a grazing area in the national forest—forest that we had traveled through for miles, were still traveling through. The cattle were headed for ranches a few miles down the valley.

The drive was not a pleasant one. The road was under construction, and the cattle kicked up a cloud of gritty dust that they and the riders breathed. Hunters were driving up to the forests in a lively succession of trucks and campers; cattle meeting them tried to turn back. Some of the cattle seemed almost frantic as they ran back and forth. Many of them were moving so fast that they were losing pounds in weight—pounds that can mean the difference in profit and loss when the cattle are marketed. The riders looked tired and hot and dirty, hard put to keep the cattle moving ahead at an easy pace.

We saw sheep on the move, too, all the time we were in the mountains. There were bands of them along the main roads and on the back roads and on the hillsides, all moving down. There were huge trucks loaded with sheep, running on roads from mountains to farms and ranches in the "lower country." Westerners have learned not to sound their car horns at a truckload of sheep or cattle; the blowing horn makes the stock crowd over to the far side of the truck—and the truck turns over.

GRAZING IS HERE TO STAY

So much has been said about the misuse of grazing lands in the West that when you say "grazing" to almost anyone, he thinks "overgrazing." Many people think that all grazing on national forests is overgrazing, and should be—is being—entirely stopped. On the other side of the coin, many people think that the Forest Service interferes unnecessarily with grazing, and so meat prices go up. Some Westerners feel that limiting national-forest grazing has ruined ranchers that depended upon it. Others remember disastrous floods that destroyed lives and homes and fields—floods that brought mud and rocks down from vulnerable watersheds where sheep and cattle had grazed heavily, perhaps had "made a fortune" for their owner.

In all of America's development, the problem of getting rangeland for livestock has been a bitter one; it still is. The average rancher, come summer, moves his stock from his ranch to summer pasture—cattle into the hills, sheep into the rugged "high country." While they're away from his ranch, he grows hay on his fields and meadows and stores it to feed them in winter. A few ranchers own lands in the mountains for summer pasture; but most of them rely on the national forests for at least part of their summer grazing. If a forest closes to grazing, the ranchers then have no place to put their stock in summer, while winter feed grows. So any decision to lessen grazing on a forest has a serious effect on every rancher using it. He is very likely to fight tooth and nail against any such decision.

How widespread is this problem—does it exist only in parts of a few western states? Just how much grazing is there in national forests today?

Grazing is permitted on national-forest lands in thirty-nine of our states. It is an important use on more than 100 million acres of forests and national grasslands—about four million acres of grasslands, which, like the forests, are managed by the Forest Service. There are nineteen national grasslands. A big one is the Little Missouri in North Dakota, where more than a million acres help to feed 50,000 cattle every year. Scattered through Texas, Oklahoma, and New Mexico, six units are grouped together as the Panhandle National Grasslands. Their 300,000 acres will

carry nearly 20,000 cattle. These are lands whose primary use is grazing.

Look, as well, at the grazing records of some of the "average" national forests. More than 7,500 head of black Angus and white-face mothers and their calves feed on the Ouachita National Forest in Arkansas and Oklahoma. From the Rocky Mountains west, grazing is a major load on nearly every forest; in New Mexico, for example, 28,000 cattle graze on the Gila National Forest, and in Idaho, 19,000 cattle and 97,000 sheep graze on the Sawtooth. These are only a small part of the total numbers that feed on the national forests.

They are owned by thousands of ranchers and farmers—so many that average ownership in some areas is less than thirty head of stock per rancher. A fairly widespread average that includes some of the heaviest grazing may reach 200 head for each rancher. Where, then, is that fabled ruthless cattle baron who

Lush mountain meadows feed thousands of sheep. This one is on Dixie National Forest, in Utah.

grew rich by gutting the public lands with his countless herds? He isn't. He has gone forever, but he has left some tough problems to today's grazers of stock. He has left some grazing lands that he overgrazed so badly that they have not yet recovered. He has left some bitter memories of his ruthlessness. He has left a tendency in most of us to be suspicious of any stockman's use of the forest.

Yet, in general, the people who are using a forest today have owned their farms and ranches near it for many years and are as much interested in protecting and developing it as any other citizen of the community. Throughout these years, they have depended on the national forest for pasturage; their way of life is built around it. And they, in turn, make up a substantial part of the suppliers of meat for this country. It is not likely that they will be turned out of the forests overnight.

Can grazing on the national forest be managed so that the forest will not be "unraveled" by it? The Forest Service is proving that it can be, and, moreover, that the grazing itself can be greatly improved.

To graze his stock on the forest, a rancher gets a permit from the district ranger. The permit states the number of stock, the fee, the part of the forest to be used, and the time that the stock can stay on it.

None of this is guesswork. The district ranger knows in advance how many head of cattle and sheep the grass in his forest will carry safely. He knows what part of the forest can safely be used for grazing, and what part is vulnerable to erosion. He knows when stock should be moved out, to leave enough grass so that it can "come back" for another season. How does he know?

In the past few years, range management has developed a system of analyzing the grazing on a forest. Aerial photographs, then maps, are made of the forest; grassy and shrubby areas are

Range maps of every forest are a part of range management.

charted. All the details of interest to grazing are noted—the kinds of grasses and shrubs and where they grow, how dense they are, how fast they can renew themselves, once they are grazed; the kind of soil; how steep the slope; the location of the nearest water; the presence of rodents, such as gophers, that can destroy grass and cause erosion with their tunnels.

Here, again, infrared sensors are coming into use; the sensors, flown over the range, can detect many of the details under study. They can photograph and identify plants, animal tracks, rodent activity, ant hills. They speed the study of animal communities and wildlife habitats, measure the use of grass by grazing animals, and report changes in vegetation and soil. The speed and accuracy with which they can do all this are a great advantage to the range manager, who must thoroughly know his range.

Sagebrush is sometimes plowed out, and good forage grasses are planted to replace it.

Juniper trees being removed in Arizona, for seeding to range grasses.

The Forest Service has learned a great deal about the different kinds of grasses—where and how they grow and their value as forage. A range manager works as hard to improve the grass on his range as he does to control grazing. He knows that while one kind of grass may produce several hundred pounds of feed per acre, a better kind may produce several thousand; and he plants and cultivates to develop the better kind. He kills weeds that cattle won't eat and other weeds that are poisonous to stock, and replaces them with good forage plants.

When vegetation adds up to a dangerous low in any area, the range manager moves grazing off of it for a time, "resting" it for a year or maybe two years, while the grass comes back. There are probably other areas that he uses the same way, rotating the stock from one to another and letting some of the areas rest while the others are being grazed. So a substantial part of the range is in use every year.

While better grass is being developed, other improvements on the forest also increase safe grazing. Fifty thousand miles of fences keep stock in areas where there is grass and keep them off vulnerable slopes. Trails, often fenced, lead to grass that animals could not or would not reach by themselves. Cattle won't go more than about two miles from water to look for food, and so tend to overgraze near water. So small reservoirs are often built to provide water where it is scarce, and watering tanks with pipelines running to them have been installed on many ranges; there are nearly 40,000 of them on the national forests. These improvements are usually built by the ranchers from materials supplied by the Forest Service.

On the Beaverhead National Forest in southern Montana, you can travel the Ruby River-Gravelly Mountain Range and see for yourself what is being done to improve grazing and at the same time protect watersheds and other forest resources. Here the Forest Service has developed a range tour of sixty miles over

A rancher and a forester inspect a range in California. This fine range was developed by a Forest Service program of erosion control and range restoration.

mountains and through valleys—a five-hour drive that makes twenty-three stops at important features. There are times when the steep grade demands the attention of everyone traveling it, including the driver's, and times when everyone stops thinking about grazing to watch a moose, a herd of pronghorns, or perhaps a black bear. But everyone sees, too, at close hand, the problems of grazing and the answers the Forest Service is developing. This exhibit holds out the important promise that grazing on the national forests is a growing resource, not a diminishing one.

FORESTS ARE FOR LEARNING

"One of the boys who helped build this room didn't know what an inch was, when he came here."

The director of the Ouachita Civilian Conservation Center on

Ouachita National Forest was showing us the new Center Headquarters Building near Royal, Arkansas. Under the supervision
of experienced craftsmen, he told us, the Center's boys had built
it, from its landscaped grounds to the last brush of varnish on
woodwork.

We looked around the attractive room and knew for sure that
when that boy had finished, he not only knew what an inch was,
but also a half, a quarter, an eighth, a sixteenth, a thirty-second.
Paneled walls glowed softly, each panel straight and matched
with its neighbors. Polished trim outlined every door and window, its corners mortised perfectly, its edges sleek and neat.
Floor tiles were square, doors were hung "true." No one could
have done this work—could even have helped with it—who could
not measure.

The room was one of several offices in a building set among
trees and surrounded by a low wall of native stone. Part of the
building's walls, too, were stone. The boys who had built this had
learned to work with mortar and stone and concrete as well as
with wood.

There are well over a hundred Corpsmen at the Center—boys
who, for the most part, have had little schooling and are unable
to hold a better job than unskilled manual labor. They sign up
for eighteen months or two years; they live at the Center, which
has a Forest Service director, and go out from it to work on the
forest with Forest Service supervisors.

They build picnic grounds and campgrounds, crafting the
stoves and building the tables. They build roads. We went up
to a new scenic road they were building to the Lake Ouachita
vista on Hickory Nut Mountain, and watched them work. They
had two big power shovels going, and a bulldozer, with two Job
Corpsmen and an instructor on each one. Up ahead was a blast-
ing rig. This is a point where the mountain is many-layered
sandstone, and the road climbing it had to be blasted out of solid

rock. The wide swath of roadbed that the boys had wrested from this unfriendy surface was impressive; later stages of road-building would soon bring a fine highway here.

We asked the Center's director for a list of the trades the boys were learning, and he came up with carpentry, masonry, welding, mechanics, use and maintenance of heavy equipment, plant maintenance and, of all things, general cooking. We had a chance to sample their cooking when they invited us to lunch at their cafeteria, and we found it superb. We asked their "head chef" if he liked cooking. He said: "I'm hooked for life. When I get through here, I can get a job cooking anywhere." He has learned to bake—can make a wedding cake—and to cook meats in a wide variety of ways, to keep vegetables fresh and colorful, to make tasty soups.

Other lines of work keep the Center humming. The boys write and print their own newspaper. They make many of the colorful and helpful signs that are all over the national forests, and they make some of the dioramas and other exhibits in the visitor centers. They do their own repair work on machines, big and little. And they are always ready to provide trained manpower in such emergencies as flood, fire, and tornado.

Much of the Center itself was built by Corpsmen. It includes an administration building for offices, a kitchen and mess hall, classrooms and a library, dormitories, and a lodge with a huge fireplace and television, radio, stereo, movie, and other recreation facilities. Tool, woodworking, and paint shops, used for the work of the forest, become hobby centers in the boys' off-duty hours. There is an athletic field; and, with the Center located on a quiet stretch of the Ouachita River, there is a big pier with accompanying boating, swimming, and fishing.

In addition to their training for a trade, the Corpsmen—formerly the Job Corps—receive schooling in "the three R's"—reading, writing, and arithmetic—and training in study skills,

Water holes such as this benefit wildlife as well as stock.

working together, personal health, and other education that they need in order to succeed in a job and to advance. After graduating from the Center, they can take a "General Education Development" exam; passing it, they receive a diploma that most colleges and universities will accept as evidence of a high-school education.

So the Job Corpsman can continue his education by going to college. If he decides to get a job instead, he is recommended by the Center on the basis of the work he has accomplished, with a resumé of his qualifications that includes an exact record of his work and an appraisal of him by the Center. The Corpsman himself receives a copy of this resumé.

In a typical case, the boy had dropped out of school after seventh grade and had no previous work experience. His resumé recorded the number of hours he had worked at the Center to qualify in carpentry and construction and showed his rating: "Good." In appraisal, it read: "He has made good progress in his basic education program. He has advanced approximately three public school grades in reading and one grade in basic math. He also completed the Center driver-education course and attained his state driver's license. He has performed in an excellent manner, has received promotions to Corpsman Specialist, and Corpsman Leader, and was awarded a merit raise for performance in work, education, and residential living. He is prompt, dependable, and ambitious to improve his educational and vocational skills. He should be very successful in a job for which he is qualified."

There are twenty Civilian Conservation Centers on national forests in fifteen states from coast to coast, serving more than

Good grazing management protects the banks of streams where they might erode. Here, grazing and fishing are two uses of the forest that do not conflict with each other.

3,500 young men. Many of these centers have agreements with labor organizations to help find jobs for their graduates.

The Corpsmen have no corner on using the forests as a place to learn. Learning is widespread on any forest. Nature trails are everywhere, to pass on to hikers the lore of plants and animals; signs interpret the life of an area, its history, its surroundings. On some forests there are special demonstration areas, such as the Alvin Creek area on Nicolet National Forest in Wisconsin, and the Lower Michigan Miniature Forest on Manistee, that offer visitors a close-up view of typical growth and management.

In California, entire elementary-school classes sometimes move into a schoolhouse on the forest, to study it at first hand for a week or more. In many places, classes in geology study such spots as Flaming Gorge in Utah, slide areas in Wyoming and Montana, and the towering cliffs of Colorado's mountains.

MINING IN THE FORESTS

Mining is another use made of the national forests that is almost as widespread and in as great variety as the forests themselves. Do you wear a gold ring on your finger? The gold may have come from a mine on a national forest high in the Rocky Mountains. Do flagstones form a path around your house or make steps in a park where you walk? They could have come from a quarry on a national forest. The natural gas in your cook stove, the gasoline in your automobile tank, the sodium in the salt you eat— any of these could have started to you from a national forest.

They come from mineral "claims" that may be owned by an individual or a company; or the claim may be leased from the government, or it may be operated under a special-use permit.

In the early days of western development, when most of the land was owned by the government, thousands of people "staked" claims on lands where there were valuable minerals. They actually staked out the boundaries of every claim, and then worked on it and spent money developing it to the point where they "patented" it—and thereafter owned both the land and the minerals underground. When national forests were established around these claims, they were not affected; land and minerals were still owned by the people who had patented them. Many of them continued to be worked through the years, and are still operated. A famous example is the Camp Bird mine above Ouray, Colorado, where gold worth millions on millions of dollars has been mined throughout this century, and is still being mined.

There are many like it, in the "hard-rock" mining country of the mountains. The miners buy lumber for their buildings from the forests around them. They use water from the forest streams. By special-use permit, they have roads across the forest to reach the mine. For their part, they are required to safeguard the forest as they use it—to keep the cutting of timber in accordance with safe use; to dispose of the "tailings" from their smelters—chemicals and waste rock and soil—in some other way than dumping them into streams.

Mining goes much farther on the forests than yesterday's claims. A prospector today can—and does—look on a forest for everything from gold to oil. If he plans to drill a well or do much digging, he gets a special-use permit from the Forest Service. If he is merely going to look, or test rock samples, or run a shovelful of gravel through his gold pan, he does not need a permit. If he finds gold, he can stake a claim and proceed to patent it, as the pioneers did. If he finds oil or gas, he can lease the right to pump it out, paying rent and royalty. If he takes out gravel or stone, he buys it on a special-use permit. There are more than 17,000 mineral leases and permits in use on the forests; hundreds of applications for new ones are received each year.

The quarrying of fine flagstone is on the increase in Arizona and the rest of the Southwest. Mining for gold continues to challenge mountain prospectors. And drilling for oil and gas is

Many strange formations are offered for study in the Sheep Creek Canyon Geological Area of Ashley National Forest, Utah.

a major activity—on the Panhandle National Grasslands; on the forests of Utah and Wyoming; on the Allegheny National Forest in Pennsylvania, only a few miles from where oil was first discovered. Successful recovery of all these minerals and many others adds up to a major resource of our forests.

MANY SPECIAL USES

Thousands of special-use permits on the national forests allow people to utilize them in a surprising number of ways. The Forest Service counts eighty different uses that are permitted; several hundred permits in a single forest are not unusual. Pipelines cross the forest, and power lines, and telephone lines, and highways; there are radio and television antenna sites. There are

The famous old Camp Bird Mine near Ouray, Colorado, is surrounded by national forest, and the road to it crosses the forest.

hundreds of group camps built on the forests, and observatories and tracking stations, rifle ranges and cemeteries, even a city park or two. There are resorts and ski areas and hunting and fishing camps. All of these operate under special-use permits, and each permit is based on opening the uses of the forest to a greater number of people.

On Florida's Apalachicola National Forest, a picnic center for handicapped people has just been opened on one of the lakes. Nature trails are built with ramps instead of steps, so that wheelchairs can travel them, and special docks and an easily reached beach and lake provide boating, swimming, sunning, and fishing. Camping facilities are in plans for the future.

The television series "Lassie" was filmed on national forests from the Gifford Pinchot in southern Washington to the Ocala in Florida. And important reserch for the moon landing was carried out by astronauts in the lava beds on national forests in central Oregon.

Christmas trees come in large numbers from national forests all over the country. Many of them are grown under power lines, where trees cannot be allowed to grow tall. Sometimes the grower is the Forest Service, and the trees are sold for an average dollar apiece to individuals. Sometimes the planting is done under special-use permit by commercial growers, who harvest the trees and ship them to market.

We saw a fantastic "harvest" come off the Apalachicola. We went out to watch the worm "grunters," people who do their harvesting in the early, gray dawn. To find them, we drove for miles over forest roads to a wide, open area near a river, where the soil was moist but not really muddy—not wet-muddy. If there is too much water, nothing happens.

The "grunters" came here in twos and threes, but mostly in families—parents, teenagers, small fry. Each party literally "staked out" its own claim, driving sturdy wooden stakes into the earth. Then everybody grabbed a strap-like piece of iron and rubbed it across a stake. The rubbing had the appearance of a strange ritual, and made a noise like a big hog grunting. Were these people trying to wring music—or something—out of the ground?

They certainly were—and did. Immediately out of the soil came great worms, six to twelve inches long. A few came first, then quantities. They crawled and writhed on top of the ground, their bodies wet and shining, the ground alive with them.

Most of the grunters left their posts and scrambled to snatch up the worms and put them in containers. If a worm was still not all the way out of the soil when touched, it snapped back underground as if it had been stabbed by a red-hot needle. But in a minute it was out again, pushed by vibrations of the stakes. Rubbing the stakes makes them vibrate; the vibrations reach into the soil; when the soil vibrates, the worms make for the surface.

The containers, from gallon-size up, filled slowly, but fill they did, and the grunters took home gallons and gallons of worms. They sell them for fish bait, for as much as a dollar per hundred. The worms run about 500 to a gallon, and the grunters pay the Forest Service five cents a hundred—a small reminder that this

At many places in America, people can pan gravel and sift out small flecks of gold from it. These campers on the Chugach National Forest in Alaska are panning on Resurrection Creek.

is your land as well as theirs, where they are harvesting.

Delicious edibles come from the forest. Huckleberries and blackberries are marvelous crops; picked by the bushel on the forest by thousands of people, they appear in pies and bottled jams on roadside stands. In the Southwest, pinyon nuts are gathered by the Indians and sold to stores and tourists. In the Chippewa National Forest in Minnesota, wild rice is harvested by Indians and others who will follow the rules—but the only legal way to harvest it is by the primitive methods early developed by the Indians.

Spaghnum moss is harvested in Oregon, peat moss in Colorado; ferns and decorative branches are gathered in almost any forest; where there are enough, lovely manzanita branches are cut in California. Cedar fence posts come from the forest in many localities, and so does firewood. On the Ocala, in Florida, thick-brushed rosemary is cut and lashed to the roofs of nurseries to provide shade, and sweet bay is gathered for seasoning and for scenting candles. On the Apalachicola, beekeepers stand in line to "pasture" their bees in the tupelo swamps, where the sweet nectar of the tupelo tree makes an unusually fine grade of honey.

Some of these harvests are free for the taking, but many require pay by volume, or a special-use permit for which the user pays a fee. They are, says the forester, with a grin, "our nickel-and-dime business." Minor they are, but foresters estimate that they generate more than $100 million in local business every year.

Probably more important than the money from them is the effect they have on the lives of the people using the forests. And this becomes more important all the time, as more and more "wild" land is tamed by fields and factories, cities and homes—as there are fewer and fewer places to pick blackberries and chokecherries, to gather wild ferns and pine cones.

Through all these many channels, the usefulness of the national forests grows and grows, until they reach, in one way or another nearly everyone. It is almost certain that you are among the thousands of lucky ones who soon will camp—or have already camped—or have hiked, hunted, fished, or skied on the national forests. It is almost certain that today, tomorrow, next day, some use of the national forest will reach out and touch you—bring you water or something made of wood, bring you electricity or a telephone call, give you beef, lamb, wool.

Look around you, and you cannot fail to find many things that bring you close to the lands of many uses.

FOR FURTHER READING

American Forests. The Magazine of Forests, Soil, Water, Wildlife, and Outdoor Recreation. American Forestry Association.

Brooks, Maurice. *The Life of the Mountains.* (Our Living World of Nature.) McGraw-Hill, 1967.

Collingwood, G. H., and Brush, Warren D. *Knowing Your Trees.* (Revised and edited by Devereux Butcher.) American Forestry Association, 1964.

Feininger, Andreas. *Trees.* Viking, 1968.

Freeman, Orville L., and Frome, Michael. *The National Forests of America.* G. P. Putnam's Sons in association with Country Beautiful Foundation, Inc., 1968.

Frome, Michael. *Whose Woods These Are: The Story of the National Forests.* Doubleday, 1962.

Grimm, William Carey. *The Book of Trees.* Stackpole, 1962.

Hillary, Louise. *Keep Calm If You Can.* Doubleday, 1964.

McCormick, Jack. *The Life of the Forest.* (Our Living World of Nature.) McGraw-Hill, 1966.

——*The Living Forest.* Harper, in cooperation with the American Museum of Natural History, 1959.

Olson, Sigurd F., and Blacklock, Les. *The Hidden Forest.* Viking, 1969.

Platt, Rutherford. *The Great American Forest.* Prentice-Hall, 1965.

Silvics of Forest Trees of the United States. Agriculture Handbook No. 271. Prepared by the Division of Timber Management Research, Forest Service. Forest Service, U.S. Department of Agriculture, 1965.

United States Department of Agriculture. *Outdoors USA.* United States Government Printing Office, 1967.

——*Trees.* United States Government Printing Office, 1949.

203

The regional offices of the U.S. Forest Service will supply much additional information. Addresses:

Alaska Region, Federal Office Building, P.O. Box 1628, Juneau, Alaska 99801.

California Region, 630 Sansome Street, San Francisco, California 94111.

Eastern Region, 710 North Sixth Street, Milwaukee, Wisconsin 53203.

Intermountain Region, 324 25th Street, Ogden, Utah 84401.

Northern Region, Federal Building, Missoula, Montana 59801.

Pacific Northwest Region, 319 Southwest Pine Street, P. O. Box 3623, Portland, Oregon 97208.

Rocky Mountain Region, Federal Center, Building 85, Denver, Colorado 80225.

Southern Region, 50 Seventh Street NE., Atlanta, Georgia 30323.

Southwestern Region, 517 Gold Avenue SW., Albuquerque, New Mexico 87101.

INDEX

Page numbers in *italics* indicate pages on which illustrations appear.